Chasing Infinity

Essays on the Nature of God, the Universe, and Religious Experience

By Michelle Belanger

Chasing Infinity, first published in 2010
by Emerald Tablet Press, Cleveland, Ohio.

ISBN: 1453722335

Table of Contents

Introduction

Most people know me for my work on vampires. If you've not encountered my writing on psychic vampirism and the modern vampire community, then it's likely that you know me as a paranormal investigator and psychic/medium for the show *Paranormal State.* I've written a number of books recently on hauntings and ghosts, but the paranormal is only one branch of interest for me. More than a ghost-hunter, more than a psychic or energy worker, I have first and foremost considered myself a scholar, and my academic background is in the realm of comparative religious studies.

The collection you hold in your hands represents over a decade's worth of articles and essays devoted to faith, religion, and the nature of God. Many of these are writings from my undergraduate days, written between 1992 and 1996. During this time, comparative religions and the nature of mystical experience were topics of particular interest for me. Several of the works you will encounter here were presented as papers during my years at John Carroll, including my senior thesis on shamanism as a variety of mystical experience. Only a few of the articles collected here were produced later than 2001 and very few of these works have been previously (or widely) published. A few lived for a little while on the House Kheperu website, kheperu.org, populating its pages in the early days of its existence.

For fans of my current work, many of these articles may seem a little rough as a consequence. My writing style has definitely changed over the years, and in many ways, I feel that I've learned to make my writing more accessible. I have considered rewriting at least a few of the articles here, and yet I feel there is more value in demonstrating a progression – not only in my writing style but also in my personal attitudes and beliefs.

The works collected here show a side of my writing and philosophies that many fans of my popular books may have never suspected of me. Since 2004, I have published books on vampires and psychic phenomenon, ghosts and demons, and while my spiritual beliefs are woven within and throughout all of these works, I have rarely given voice exclusively to the insights and theories that led me to those beliefs. The articles in this book, then, are collected in part to show the process of my own journey of belief. The articles are also collected together in order to show the importance of those beliefs – not only how they were shaped and developed, but why belief has always been a topic of interest and importance to me.

It is my hope that in sharing these early works, I will not only shed some light on my current attitudes and philosophies, but that I will also inspire my readers to consider more profoundly the nature and origins of their own beliefs.

Michelle Belanger

July 21, 2010

Infinitude

Imagine that God is the ocean and you are a water glass. If you dip the glass into the ocean, it is the ocean that fills the vessel.

It is in you. It *is* you.

However, the glass cannot contain everything that is in the ocean. The ocean holds vast diversity, and a water glass can only contain a small portion of this.

So there is much more to the ocean than what fills the glass, even though the water in the glass and the water in the ocean are parts of the same thing.

If we were all poured out into a larger vessel, the ocean would be greater still. Yet each of us contains a portion of infinity.

Religion, Spirituality, and Truth

As a student of comparative religion, I devoted a good portion of my undergraduate and graduate studies to learning about the religious and mystical systems of the many world traditions. A wonderful professor, Dr. Paul Nietupski, taught wide-ranging classes on comparative religions at my *alma mater*, John Carroll. The two most comprehensive and enlightening classes that I had the pleasure of attending were Pilgrimage (an introductory level course which was nevertheless very profound and challenging) and Mysticism (a graduate level class comprised of about ten very intelligent and very articulate people who each got a chance to lead the class in exploring a different tradition).

In both of these courses, a point was driven home to me that I had already strongly suspected: every system, every religion, is founded on the same fundamental beliefs. The symbols that represent them may vary, and the doctrines built around the core of beliefs certainly vary as well, but the basic religious truths remain the same. These truths, in many ways, are a simple product of human existence. As thinking beings, we are not content to simply live, eat, reproduce, and die. We wonder where we came from and where we may go. We wonder if there is any purpose to our lives beyond surviving and reproducing. We wonder if that particular consciousness we know as "I" will exist in an unaltered form after our bodies have turned to dust. We wonder if there is anything bigger than us out there that may be directing the whole show. Endlessly, we wonder.

And the answers we develop from these musings become religion. Whether we answer these questions out of a deep-seated psychological need to create order and purpose when there really is none, or whether we answer them because there is indeed some greater purpose and pattern to it all and we somehow inherently sense this, really doesn't matter. The truth is, until we die, we can know nothing for certain about these things. Until then, we can only wonder, speculate and believe. How or why we have created religious thinking among our species is not what's important. The fact that such thinking exists, combined with the fact that it is largely identical in every time, in every culture, in every ethnic group and on every continent is what I find really striking.

Now, we can chalk up the basic universality of religion to pure human psychology. As humans, our minds all operate on similar principles and in similar ways, therefore it might even be remarkable if our religious thinking did *not* have a universal thread of similarity running through it. Despite the variety of our individual experiences, we still, on a fundamental level, share the same pattern to our lives: we are born, we live, we mature, we find mates, sometimes we raise children, we grow old, we die. When we sleep, we dream, thus proving to us that our minds can sometimes continue on despite our conscious use of them. Our sense of the distinction between mind and body allows us to posit the existence of a soul. And in the natural world, the seasons go through a definite cycle of creation, death, and renewal, thus leading us to conclude that perhaps by extension this same cycle affects all things, including the soul.

So what are the basic universal truths that lie at the core of every religion? I've touched upon them a little above, but let me lay them out here as I perceive them:

First, we believe that we are more than just bodies. There is something greater to what we think of as "I" than just flesh and blood. This, of course, is our belief in the soul.

Second, we believe that this soul, being more than just the body, is not limited like the body. The body ages and eventually dies. We perceive the soul as something ageless and immortal, something which can carry on our unique Selves beyond the death of the body.

Third, we believe that there is a greater purpose to existence than simply basic survival and reproduction. This is somewhat connected to the belief in the soul, because why would we have a soul which made us more than just our physical bodies if there were no purpose to life beyond the functions of those physical bodies? We are aware of the soul, and thus there must be something more. As we believe that the soul is eternal, by extension, we must assume that this something more is in some way concerned with eternal things, things which exist outside of and beyond the limits of the body.

Fourth, we posit the existence of an intelligent force that accounts for that "something more" beyond the physical limits of the body. Most religions tell us that the soul is in fact a small portion of this intelligent force, and that it is from this connection to that force that the soul gets its eternal and undying qualities. This force is seen as something greater than anything we can imagine, something so vast that it encompasses all of creation itself, and yet still manages to be more. Some religions humanize this force, give it a name, a personality: they call it "God". Other religions do not even dare to give it a name or a face, acknowledging that it is too big for their limited human imaginations to even conceive. They acknowledge its existence, but they allow it to be this vast, unknowable thing that may or may not be conscious as we understand consciousness, but which has always been and will always be there, behind the scenes, fueling the cycles of reality.

This is the one fundamental point where religions differ: the expressed nature of God. But even if the divine force is never given a face or a name, the general principle remains the same: there is something greater than we ourselves, and it is behind all the mysterious things in the universe that we do not understand and may never be able to know.

Now, as discussed above, the doctrines and organizational structures, the ethical and moral invectives, all of these things which contribute to an *organized* religion vary greatly. And oftentimes, these other structures are built up in so many dense and complex layers over the original grain of truth that it is very hard to see the similarities between, say, Islam and Wicca, Shinto and Catholicism. This is one reason why the class on mysticism was so important to this realization of mine. Every religion has two aspects: there is the lay religion, which is the truth as interpreted for the masses, and then there is the esoteric or mystical tradition, which is the Truth that only a select few of the religious elite can really grasp.

I generally make the distinction by calling the lay-truth "religion" and the elite Truth "spirituality". Religion is the truth presented in such a way that just about any one can grasp it and feel a connection to it. They may only be scratching the surface, and many of the more mysterious and hard to grasp concepts will be massively simplified (if not outright swept under the rug). But the basics are there for anyone to learn. Additionally, religion defines a person's belief system for them, so they don't have to put the effort into developing it on their own. It also tells them exactly how to integrate that belief system into their daily lives as far as ethics and moral behavior are concerned. Basically, religion is the *Cliff's Notes* for people who don't have the time, the understanding, or the inclination to delve deeper and wrestle with more profound, more personal meanings.

Spirituality on the other hand is the independent study project undertaken by one adventurous and gifted individual. In spirituality, there is no safety net where things are easily defined for you. You cannot be satisfied with just scratching the surface, and you cannot be satisfied with just taking the answers you are handed. You need to explore all the aspects of the belief system in order to fully understand them in your own context. You need direct, personal experience of the Truths that the religion is based upon in the first place.

In religious lingo, striving toward spirituality as opposed to just following a religion makes you a mystic. Each and every religious system the world over has a mystical tradition which comprises the esoteric part of that belief system. And while the mystical system usually makes a passing nod to the culturally and temporally defined symbols and structures of the religion it has come from, its real aim is toward what lies beneath these. And it is in the mystical system, where oftentimes the overt (and mainly superficial) layers of the religion have been stripped away, that you can really see the commonalties of all belief systems.

Here is where the Truth of human religion comes out: not in the doctrine and dogma produced by established "church leaders," but in the writings of visionaries and mystics such as the Muslim Dervish Rumi, the Christian Saint Theresa of Avila, the Hindu practitioner of Kundalini Yoga, Gopi Krishna, the Hermeticist Isha Schwaller de Lubicz, the Renaissance visionary Giordano Bruno, plus numerous practitioners of the Qabbalah, the shamans, the ascetics, the magicians, yogis and seers: the marginalized, the heretical, and the revered. And nearly all of these visionaries develop systems which explode the cultural and temporal boundaries of religion. When they see the Truth, they also see the universal reality of that Truth, and suddenly the differences between Christ and Krishna, Allah and Amaterasu are perceived to be nothing more than conceptual boundaries humanity has built for itself. The overt symbol systems that usually tend to divide and confuse people are revealed as nothing more than window dressing, and the mystic's vision pierces those curtains to see what they really hide.

It should come as no surprise that practically every mystic the world over has, upon achieving their vision, striven toward religious tolerance and education. In seeing past the boundaries themselves, they have then devoted much of their lives and their writings to helping others see that those boundaries shouldn't even exist. Of course, time and culture, and the persistence of lay religion always conspire against them and keep people ideologically apart, but they always reach a few. And their writings are accessible across cultural boundaries. Anyone in the Christian West can pick up Rumi's poetry and find something which they relate to, even though he is writing from within a religion that is engaged in an ideological struggle with Christianity that is so deep and emotionally charged, it should be considered a religious war.

Regardless of the costume our religion wears or the names we give our gods, the Truth is there. It is the same for everyone. We are born, we grow, we age, we die, and we believe that there is more to it than that. We believe that there is a greater purpose and that the real point of life is to discern this purpose, and to perhaps come into direct personal contact with that immense force which is a part of that purpose. Call it Allah or Yahweh, Gaia or God, those are just words to make it a little more conceptually accessible to us. Take the words away, and there is a secret which all humanity shares. And that secret is what makes each of us greater than these vessels of flesh.

The Many Faces of God(dess)

In October 1994, I was involved in a hand-fasting ceremony. For those unfamiliar with the term, a hand-fasting is basically the Wiccan and neo-Pagan version of a wedding. The hand-fasting was between two students of John Carroll University who were both Pagan. John Carroll, it should be mentioned, is a Jesuit Catholic university. Because the couple being handfasted were students, however, they were allowed to use the college's chapel for a relatively low fee, and so the Pagan ceremony was to take place in what was essentially a Catholic church.

The resident priest had taken care to remove any consecrated Eucharists from the Tabernacle as well as any other items that were specifically sacred to his beliefs, but otherwise, we had free run of the place for our ritual. The school had even been so kind as to provide us access to the sacristy of the chapel for use as a changing room for the bride. While back there, I couldn't help but look through the various bits of Catholic paraphernalia stored on counters and shelves. The censers, the candelabras, the chalices, the wine... I was struck by the almost generic nature of the ritual items. Aside from the cross and other obviously Christian symbols stamped on the chalice and even the priests' vestments, these could have been the ritual tools in any number of non-Christian temples – including my own home altar. In my office of priestess, I owned a censer identical to that I saw tucked away in this Catholic sacristy. The candles, the chalice, even the robes (unless the group insisted on doing things ritually naked or "skyclad") could have easily been part of a Wiccaning or even the hand-fasting that afternoon. The words of the rituals and ostensibly the gods which they invoked differed, but the tools of ritual seemed very much the same.

That got me to thinking. When most Christians want something from God, they give voice to their needs, and then they light candles. Pagans and Wiccans do the same thing, lighting candles and speaking aloud or to themselves the thing that they desire. To Christians, this is prayer. To Pagans, it is magick. When the Christians (and members of many other faiths) pray, they are seeking the aid of a deity outside of themselves to affect their lives in a positive way. Pagans, through magick, are seeking to harness the power of the deity within in order effect change. And yet the essence of the activity is the same. Both frequently use candles as a focus, a concrete representation of a spiritual desire. Both solemnly speak their need aloud or reflectively focus on it in silence. Sometimes incense is burned – and it both cases, this is both an offering and a symbol which carries the essence of the need upward, with the smoke, to the heavens.

Christians often see Wicca and neo-Paganism as wholly antithetical to their faith, and yet both belief systems recognize the existence of God, the immortality of the soul, and the deeper meaning to our lives beyond mere material gain. The name of the God differs, the outward trappings of ritual differ, yet underneath it all, the religious sentiment is nearly identical.

As a minister who serves the Wiccan and neo-Pagan communities in my area, I think I am more poignantly aware of this than many others. The very nature of the religion(s) which my office serves can best be described as multi-faceted. The fundamental thrust of neo-Paganism lies in its belief that religious belief and experience is a wholly personal thing.

However, let me qualify that statement. The words with which one chooses to pray, the names with which one chooses to invoke the deity, the faces and guises one recognizes as those of the deity -- these all differ from person to person. This is why I may be called upon to preside over a rite consecrating a couple to Aphrodite on one day and the next be required to make an offering to Shiva with someone who recognizes the need for change in his life.

The names and faces of the deity are many; each is, in a sense, an archetypal figure which represents one aspect, one side of the ultimate divinity. Since, as limited, finite beings, we cannot comprehend the infinite which is God, we must try to comprehend it in smaller, more easily digestible pieces of the greater whole. These individual "gods" are divinities in that they are a face of the divine. The concept is difficult at first, I realize, and this is one major reason the neo-Pagan movement has been accused of polytheism. But it's important to understand that while a neo-Pagan may pray to Apollo and Odin and Cernunnos and Kwan Yin all in the same breathe, they recognize these names as separate faces of a greater whole -- but ultimately it is the whole that they pray to.

And so the outward symbols of each individual differ greatly and would seem to be irreconcilable with any other system, and yet at the very core of the belief, the goal is the same. The same is true of Hinduism; Karma Yoga and the Yoga of Renunciation are very different paths, and yet they are merely two different ways of achieving the same goal: awareness of the Atman and subsequent union with the higher power that is Brahman.

I feel that this is applicable to all religious systems. Each system has its rhetoric, its system of symbols and names and myths. The religion is then a combination of all of these things. The rites, the ceremonies, the beliefs, all of these are defined by the basic system. And yet the goal of that system, worship and a union with or, at the very least, a striving toward, the divine, is a goal shared by all religions.

It is, I argue, the fundamental nature of religion. The way in which religious experience and religious belief are expressed is influenced by the culture, the time, and the geography of a given people. As a result of these influences, the symbols seem to differ, but the underlying meaning of these symbols is a constant for every faith.

De-Mystifying Magick

Have you ever wanted to change something in your life? Perhaps you wanted to understand yourself better, but you weren't quite sure how or where to start. Perhaps a close friend had an illness and you wanted to help them toward healing. Or perhaps you needed to draw a little extra money your way to get through the end of the month.

Whenever someone wants something very much, they start wishing for it to come to them. It's such a simple, ordinary thing to do, I bet you hardly realize when you're doing it. If you are suffering from an illness, for example, you start by thinking to yourself, "I wish I were better — or at least I wish I didn't hurt so much." After a while, you start thinking about what it would be like to feel better. You envision how you would be spending your time if you weren't sick in bed. Maybe you picture the sickness as a black icky something clinging inside of you, and you imagine yourself scraping it out until it's all gone. You picture yourself healthy and happy and free of the illness, and you yearn for your wish to become reality.

And maybe sometimes it does.

Whether you know it or not, if you've done something like what I've described above, you've done magick. At least, magick is what most people call it these days. Other people call it prayer. It doesn't matter what name you call it by — magick and prayer are essentially the same thing: in both, you are calling on a higher power in order to get something done in your life. In the case of prayer, you are usually asking a higher power outside of yourself to do the miracle working. God, Jesus, Yahweh, whatever face your vision of the deity wears, that's who you direct your wishes to.

In the case of magick, the divinity you are calling upon lies within yourself. That's not to say exactly that you are a god with all the powers of a god. Although some might argue that point, it's not precisely true. God is infinite and omnipotent, and you, as an incarnate being, are finite and limited. After all, if you were a god, you wouldn't be sick in the first place. But there is a part of you that is connected to divinity, and this divine spark has power. If you call upon that power and believe that the god can move through you and within you, then you can make your own wishes come true. Either way, it is the divine that gets the job done in the end.

The real trick, in both magick and in prayer, is believing that just by asking for something, it will come to you. In traditional religion, this belief is called faith. The prayers of the faithful are answered. Why? Because the faithful truly believe that god cares enough to answer their prayers. With magick, you have to have a little faith as well. You can't just wish for something and expect it to appear — you really have to believe that by willing something to happen in your life it will.

As with everything, of course, there are rules to how these things happen. The faithful don't pray for things they know their god would never grant them. Part of faith is understanding what you can reasonably expect from the divine. If you pray for all the gold in the world to appear at your feet in ten days — even if you have the honest intention of redistributing that gold to the poor right then — you probably aren't even going to get your god's attention. There is only so much absurdity a deity will put up with.

It's the same with magick. You cannot ask the deity within yourself to achieve blatantly unreal ends. Immortality, riches beyond your wildest dreams, agonizing death to your enemies — these are just not things you should ask for if you really understand how the asking works. Also, when it comes down to it, even if you got one of these things through an odd fluke of fate, you probably would realize it wasn't worth the having once it was yours.

I know, I know — some of you are saying, "Well of course you don't ask for things like death to your enemies — there's the Rule of Three to protect against stuff like that." For those unfamiliar with it, the Rule of Three is a traditional Wiccan belief that everything you do will come back to you three times over (in some traditions its three times three over). No matter how many times it comes back to you, the basic gist of this rule is that you reap what you sow. And I'm not knocking the Rule of Three or even seeking to suggest that it's not out there and enforced by some Karmic agents on a pretty regular basis — what I'm trying to say is that if you use common sense in your workings, you never need to worry about the negative aspect of the Rule of Three. You should only ask for those things that you can reasonably expect to be given.

But how do you know what you can ask for? The simplest but most frustrating answer I have to that is this: If you are in touch with yourself and with the world around you, you just know. But what if you feel you don't know? My answer again is that you probably *do* know — you just don't trust your knowledge. But that's all right, at least for now. It's hard to trust those unspoken understandings that a lot of us have. The society we are surrounded by tells us to definitely *not* trust them. So, again, we come to the question: how do you know?

Common sense is a good guide, but let's admit it — not all of us are wise all the time. Other good guides are sincerity and humility. Your desire should always be sincere and your need should always be valid. You should never ask for something out of greed or anger or jealousy. That will get you nowhere fast. But if you truly do need something, then call for it. Try to bring it into your life. And while you are trying to call this thing to you, make certain that you believe it can and will come. Have the courage to trust that the divinity — which exists inside you, outside you, and throughout all things — will provide for your needs.

So, how do you do it? Well, when people pray, they often light candles. They sometimes speak their prayers out loud or have them written out on paper. Sometimes, a whole group of people get together to think hard about a prayer, to recite it, and to light candles to show how much they really want this prayer to shine like a beacon for the deity to see. And that's about what you do when you try to magick something into your life as well. Speak your desire. Write it out. Burn a candle and while the candle burns, look upon its light and think very intently upon your wish. Light some incense. Go to a special place where you feel more power that could bring your desire into reality. Perhaps even gather in a group and have everyone concentrate on what you need. Speak it out loud again. *Sing.*

And of course, believe in your heart of hearts that doing these things will bring what you want to you. Trust that you have the power to change your life. Know it, so for a moment, that knowledge is all you can feel.

You might not know at first whether all this worked or not. Magick is not a straightforward thing and it can take its time about getting back to you. Sometimes your will is manifested in a most roundabout way. Don't look too hard for a result right away. And don't build any expectations. I've seen a lot of people work a ritual (that's exactly what that candle-burning, thoughtful, praying bit I described above is — a ritual. Some people would call it a spell. Nothing scary or esoteric about it — in fact, its quite easy and people – even non-Wiccan people –do things like it all the time) with a certain expectation for the results planted in their skulls. And they are so busy looking for just that one way in which the ritual should be (in their minds) answered that they entirely miss the magick when it actually does come to them.

To give you an idea of how "magick works in mysterious ways", I have a story to tell. I worked with a girl who was just starting out on the Wiccan path. She was, in fact, just starting out on a lot of things, including a serious relationship and living on her own. Money was tight, as it so often is for young people starting out on their own for the first time. She asked me what she could do to help make ends meet, and particularly, she was interested in any magickal methods for this trick. I suggested a few spells, and she chose the one she liked the most and went with it. She was disappointed that nothing happened at first. I guess she was under the impression that she'd find a wad of cash lying in the street the next morning. Time passed, and I imagine she just presumed the spell didn't work at all.

Then, about two weeks after performing the spell I gave her, she was fired from her job. She was livid and scolded me for giving her such a terrible spell. It had backfired, she complained. But the day that she came into work to tell me how rotten the spell had worked, one of our regular customers came in and was talking about needing help over at her job. The kind of help she needed was exactly what the young lady was qualified for – far more qualified, I might add, than she was for the work at the previous job. The regular customer finished our conversation, with, "I like the both of you so much. It's a pity you already work here or I'd tell you to come and work for me."

Bang! That was it. The young lady was hired the next day at the new job and was making nearly twice there what she had made at her old occupation. But I know she didn't see that coming when she tried the spell.

It's not always a perfect scenario like the one described above, but sometimes you get wonderful results. Of course, if you perform a spell to help you find a new job, and you never actually go out and put applications in anywhere, don't expect something to fall in your lap out of nowhere. But that's just common sense, to me. You have to put a little effort into helping your desire actualize itself outside of your ritual work. But eventually, it does work, and if nothing is going right in your life at all, does it really hurt to try something unconventional?

I encourage everyone – Wiccans, Pagans, even Christians, to give magick a try. As you've seen above, anyone can do it, and it's not nearly as objectionable or as esoteric as many people make it out to be. You don't need to be an enlightened Magus with a hoary old beard and pointed cap to do magick. Most people do it everyday. The only trick is realizing that you're doing it.

The most important thing to remember — aside from using common sense in your requests — is that your personal belief is very important to the potency of the ritual. If you feel silly or stupid sitting around your room lighting candles and burning incense and chanting your wishes out loud, then stop! That approach is not for you. Only do what you're comfortable with and only do what seems to work best for you. Some people prefer plain old candle magick. Some people like to sit back, relax, and try visualizing their desires into existence. And some people think this whole spell business is pretty hokey, so they just think quietly to themselves about what they want without the aid and clutter of candles, herbs, incense, or any of that. And that's fine, too. This is not about playing sorcerer, nor is it about how strange and mysterious you can look while fiddling with your herbs and other toys. This is about your needs and desires and how you can harness the divinity within you to bring those things into reality.

Oh — and don't forget to thank that divinity once it's done its work for you. You don't need to give it a name or a face (although you're perfectly welcome to do so if that's what works for you) but you should be genuinely grateful. After all, people who just take and take and take eventually aren't given anything anymore. But that, too, is just common sense.

The Enduring Character of Sacred Sites

Every religion the world over has had certain places which it views as sacred. Holy mountains, sacred wells, blessed grottoes – shrines are built around them and pilgrimages are made to seek blessing, healing, and inspiration. Typically, these sacred sites are tied directly to the mythic system of the local religion. And yet, many of these sacred sites remain even after the religion that once revered them was supplanted by another belief system. And, intriguingly, the new religion, even if it differs radically from the old, will frequently acknowledge the self-same sites as sacred, only expressing their connection to divinity in slightly different terms.

This raises some interesting questions about the nature of a sacred site. Can a place be imbued with such qualities that, regardless of the religious system viewing it, it can still be recognized as a sacred place? Is there some quality that goes deeper than myth that makes a place sacred – and can this sacredness endure despite changing belief systems?

In Mexico, there are several shrines visited by modern Catholics that were once shrines held sacred to the local pagan gods. Lourdes is another modern sacred site with roots in Pagan antiquity, and there are several such places in Ireland. One such site, a source of hot springs, had a bath built around it and was dedicated to a Celtic goddess who the infiltrating Romans interpreted as Diana. The hot springs of the shrine provided healing baths for devotees. From items discovered at the bottom of these springs and wells, once they were healed, pilgrims returned to give thanks, making offerings of carved wood and stone representations of the cured limb or organ. When Christianity swept over Ireland, the leaders of the new religion could not erase the existence of the shrine, nor its draw to those who still sought healing from its waters, and so they merely attributed it s powers to the Virgin of their mythos. Carvings of limbs and organs that date well into the era when Christianity held sway can be found side by side with similar carvings gifted to the Pagan gods of the well.

Several of the previously mentioned Mexican shrines, integrated into the cult of the Virgin Mary, were held sacred to local deities long before the visitations of the Virgin prompted Catholics to venerate the sites. In one such case, the tree that was held sacred to the former deity still stands near the site. In other cases, sacred objects, plants, and symbols that were linked to the original (or latest) deity of the shrine were simply adopted by the Catholics and applied to their own deity. Suns, moons, roses, even the maguey plant seem to be established symbols of the sacred that were merely transferred to the new object of devotion.

How transferable is the idea of sanctity? Again, I return to Ireland and the case of St. Brighid. Brighid was a Celtic goddess of the forge, of poetry, and of inspiration. Her holy day was Candlemas, the 2nd day of February. Among the Celts, her cult was very strong and many places bear the mark of her name to attest this. When Christianity came to Ireland, the priests at first tried to stamp out the earlier cult in order to make way for their new one. Their efforts were wasted. Rather than abandoning Brighid, the local people merely worked her into the new religion. An elaborate mythos was built around her in which she became the Irish foster-mother of Christ.

As the story goes, during the travels of the holy family, the Christ child came with Mary to Ireland. Mary was called away for some time and she left her holy child in the charge of St. Brighid. The power that Brighid held over the Celts is especially evident in the fact that her story conflicts so completely with any orthodox belief in the Virgin and the childhood of Christ -- and yet, she is still accorded sainthood in defiance of these conflicts. Some of the tales concerning her have her raising the child from infancy, serving as wet nurse and mother in Mary's place. Her holy day is still observed today, and even we in the States can feel the repercussions of her cult. As modern Americans, we still celebrate groundhog day. This day, of course, falls on Candlemas, the Celtic holy day where the spring quickens beneath the snows and the first promise of new life is whispered to the cold and slumbering soil. Our furry little rodent is not running from his shadow: he is scenting the air to see if Brighid has touched the land to awaken its inner fire.

The ultimate question on the transferability of sanctity is this: is there a difference between the goddess and the saint, the vision of the Virgin or of the pagan genius loci when the end results among followers are the same? The baths appropriated by Christianity healed Pagans before and they healed Christians thereafter. The site of the visions of Guadeloupe had been a place where a Pagan goddess had appeared to the faithful centuries before Christianity came and gave her the name Mary.

When the same site is revered regardless of who is ostensibly in charge of it, doesn't the validity of its results imply something? If the powers attributed to these sites are the same, if the faith invested in them has the same impact on believers, the distinction of which god or goddess is responsible becomes a superficial consideration. The real power seems to be in the place itself. Each culture simply gives a new name to that power so they can better relate to the truth behind the name.

The Infinite Nature of Divinity

God, by very definition, is infinite. There is no single name, scripture, or doctrine that contains all of the divine truth. These systems cannot contain all of the truth nor can they contain the "only" truth because they are the creation of man, and man, unlike God, is finite and therefore fallible.

The very act of describing divinity in words limits it, and thus obscures some aspect of its divinity. At best, each system captures a small portion of the vastness of divinity, but for as much truth as any one system might possess, there is still an infinite amount of God-truth that it cannot contain. This is why every religious tradition the world over is at once partly right and partly wrong. No matter how enlightened or all-embracing the doctrine, it cannot contain the truth for every person or every situation.

This is hardly a new concept. Mystics in all times and all places have known that no single tradition can ever encompass all of the truth. As the Muslim poet, Jelaludin Rumi observes, "there are many ways to bend the knee and pray." Religions, in trying to define God, sacrifice a great deal of the truth in order to construct a doctrine. Mystics, who rise out of individual religious systems, such as Christianity, Judaism, and, in Rumi's case, Islam, shatter the barriers of doctrine and develop intensely personal spiritual paths. Rather than trying to define God, they simply experience God, and by surrendering themselves to that experience, they often come much closer to a true comprehension of the divine that moves through them and through everything around them.

When you realize that God is infinite, you also realize that no finite human authority could ever claim to know everything about God. God (the divinity, Brahmin, Goddess, the Force - whatever you want to call it, since names mean very little to something so vast - no name can truly name it without limiting it anyhow!) is the entire universe, and everything in it, and everything beyond it that cannot be sensed yet is still God. This fundamental truth was expressed best in the Qabbalah as the concept of non-duality. Non-duality is the basis for the monotheism that separated Judaism from most of the contemporary religions of its day, and yet to describe this belief as monotheism as we understand the word today is to lose a great deal of the meaning behind "non-duality."

Simply put, non-duality does not merely mean that there is only one God. It means *everything* is God. This is the truth that the mystics surrender themselves up to, becoming one with God and with all the universe in their ecstatic visions. There is only one God because there cannot be anything *but*

God in the universe. I'm God, you're God, the rocks and trees are God, even the tiniest bacteria is God. To say that God is this and not that is, according to the Qabbalah, to be dualistic. And thus, to say that the God of one system is not the self-same God of another system is essentially recognizing the existence of a different God, or at the very least something which is *not* God, and that again is duality.

What this all comes down to is the inescapable fact that every religious and spiritual tradition the world over is at least somewhat correct, and should be respected for that correctness. Not all religions are created equal for every person and every situation, however, so the wise seeker must be discerning and always seek the truth on their own. Yet a religion by its very definition is striving to understand divinity. Some seek to unify man with the divine. Some seek merely to put man in contact with a nearly unreachable God through some intermediary. Yet all religions and spiritual paths are concerned with helping the individual gain a better understanding of their Self, their relation to the world around them, and their relation with or connection to divinity.

To put it in a metaphor -- some paths might go through brambles. Some might wend their way around treacherous gullies and cliffs. Some might even meander through vast, faceless plains. Yet all are pointed toward the same destination, and all will help the diligent traveler to eventually arrive at that destination with a better understanding of his journey and himself. No one can say what path is right or wrong for any other person. All we can do is walk the path that is best for us, content in knowing that each of us will arrive in our own time and in our own way.

The Concept of Mystical Union

One of the commonalities of religious experience that can be traced across cultures is the union which the mystic feels he or she can achieve with the Divine. From St. Teresa of Avila to the Jelaluddin Rumi, mystics around the world speak of their experience of Divinity in terms of a communion or even a marriage. The soul of the mystic is seen as rising up and becoming one with divinity. In this state of union, the mystic may even identify himself with God, as, having achieved ecstatic union, he feels his earthly personality melt away and become part of the totality of the universe.

The language with which mystics typically describe their union with divinity has been largely responsible for the negative reactions they received by the mainstream religion of their particular age. St. Teresa's visions were closely investigated by the Church in order to determine whether her eloquently described "marriage" to Christ was heretical or blasphemous. St. John of the Cross saw his mystical experiences in terms of union as well, and for this the religious authorities in his native land had him thrown in prison.

In general, those who are part of the religious establishment view the mystic's notion of unmediated spiritual experience as both dangerous and presumptuous. It is dangerous because it questions the authority of the religious hierarchy set in place to serve as mediators between humanity and the divine, thus undermining the power of the priests who enforce that hierarchy. And it is presumptuous because the general contention of mainstream religious thought is that no mere mortal can *become* God – yet this is exactly what the language of mystical union frequently implies.

It seems to me that our understanding of the term "union" in a mystical context relies directly upon our definition of the soul. Generally, in any discussion on this problem, two sides emerge. On one side, the soul is defined as something which elevates us as beings and endows us with a yearning toward the divine. It is a sacred space within us, yet it is not in and of itself a piece of divinity. The other position holds that the soul is indeed a drop of the divine and it is through its presence within us that we exist in a constant state of union with the divine.

The first understanding of soul leads us to a position which maintains that it is impossible for us as humans to achieve union with the divine. The second mode of thought suggests that we are in constant union with divinity and that mystical experiences of union are not so much a sudden attainment of this union as they are a sudden and incandescent awareness of it. In the first model, we strive toward but can never truly attain a union with the divine. The second allows that we are all divine but only sometimes aware of the presence of divinity within ourselves.

I would argue for the second understanding of the nature of the soul. For any sort of mystical experience to be possible -- indeed, for us to even want to pursue it with the fervor that many of us do -- there must be a spark of the divine gleaming within us. If, as in orthodox Judaism, the divine is so far removed from humanity as to be completely untouchable, unnamable, and unattainable, why worship anything at all? What is the sense of abstractly grasping at the incomprehensible nature of a deity who is so far beyond us that we know our efforts are doomed from the start? Why enter into such an exercise of futility?

Rather, if the deity created the cosmos, as all religions I am familiar with hold, how can we not assume that there is a piece, a drop, a spark of that divinity within us? I draw upon the human example of the writer. A writer, each time he puts pen to paper, sets out to create an entire world, peopled with his own creations. And even when the creation fails and the characters do not achieve what the writer set out for them to achieve, he cannot simply crumple the sheet and go on as if those characters never once breathed, wept, and laughed somewhere within his mind.

Our creations are all extension of ourselves. This goes for noble, lovable, and intrinsically good characters as well as for the base, detestable, and intrinsically evil characters. In my experience, a writer is often more fond of his "bad guys" than his "good guys." But I digress.

My point here is to demonstrate the nature of creation. When we on a human level create, we cannot help but weave something of our being into those creations. That is what defines them as our creations: we would not have set out to create if we did not intend to imbue them with some aspect of our life, our experience, our emotions. Likewise, if the deity is indeed the first cause and creator of all things, how can it/he/she possibly have created a cosmos completely separate and distinct from itself?

Each of the characters in my novel are different parts of me. Aspects of my face and my life peer back at me from its pages. The characters certainly do not encompass all of who I am, and yet that connectedness is undeniable. There is something of me in them and every last one of them exists in a place within me. Ultimately, I am more than simply those characters. But still, a part of me exists within each of them or else they would not exist.

The case of the great creator must be an analog to this. I can see no other way for creation to have happened save for a supreme being to have drawn it all painfully, lovingly out of itself. And the result is a panentheistic universe in which everything is a part of the deity, and yet, as the supreme being, the deity is the sum of its parts and much, much more.

Religious numinosa is universal; the attainment of union is universal. I will not be so naive as to say that the *process* of achieving union is universal. This is where the fundamental distinctions occur; it is in the path that individuals vary and that the tension and differences are perceived. But while the road that one follows may wind through hills or weave along the ocean or even stretch through vast expanses of desert, the destination is the same.

Union -- the awareness of union -- is the unifying factor of mystical experience. That is why the accounts of the experience, even the metaphors and symbols used to describe it are strikingly similar across cultures. But the way in which a people achieves union, the path which they perceive, the nature of the universe which they use to define themselves and their religion, these things necessarily differ. These qualities are socially, culturally and temporally defined. Such cultural definitions cannot be avoided because the way in which we perceive ourselves, our universe and our god, is built up bit by bit through our individual experience. It is only at the apex of mystical experience that such cultural baggage falls away and we can perceive the unifying factor of the cosmos. The ways to enlightenment are many, but eventually all paths lead to the center.

Finding a Spiritual Mothertongue

As my group House Kheperu has grown both as an organization and as a concept over the past few years, our mission has grown and changed. We have been getting to know one another, and getting to understand ourselves better, and through this, we have come to better understand our path.

One thing we have seen as we study all the various religious, spiritual, and metaphysical systems that are out there is this: everyone seems to be talking about the same thing, only each in his or her own language. The reason there is friction between Pagans and Christians, New Agers and Occultists is that each thinks the other is somehow wrong, and each tends to judge on his or her own assumptions, and all of this is based on the superficialities of language.

Basically, when you belong to a system, be it an organized religion or a more amorphous spiritual path, you learn a language specific to that tradition. You and everyone else in that tradition then communicate in terms of that language. The language is different for each system, and rarely is a person from one group conversant in the language of another. And yet, once you get past the specialized terminology and the jargon unique to each group, what lies beneath are basic, universal principles.

A Christian seeks a new job, so he lights a candle and says a prayer, asking God to change reality for him. A Pagan seeks a new job, so he lights a candle and performs a spell, wherein he harnesses the God-within to change reality for him. A New Ager might put a call out to the Universe in order to get the job, envisioning white light instead of the candle.

In each case, you have a person reaching toward an aspect of divinity and seeking to change reality. Christians see God as something outside of them. Depending on the Pagan, God can be both within or without. New Agers can recognize the divinity within and, like Pagans, they might harness their internal godhood to create change, or, like Christians, they might ask the favor of the Godhood outside of themselves.

Yet all are doing the exact same thing. Only in language is it really different. For one, it is a prayer, for another it is a spell. It can be called a working, a coincidence, synchronicity, magnetizing, and any number of other specialized names. The basic principle behind the working similarly has multiple names. For one, it's religion, for another, it's magick, for another spirituality, and for still others, its metaphysics.

These different terms describe in essence the same thing, and yet a Christian may cry out against magick, and a Pagan may just as easily look down upon metaphysics. Each is judging on the superficial appearance of a word and not looking deeper to its real meaning. That's about as foolish as judging a person by the color of their skin and failing to recognize that, underneath the skin, everyone is human.

We Kheprians are a part of yet apart from all these different groups. As a result, our perspective is very different. We have to be conversant in all these different languages, and because of this, we see the meaning behind the words. Often, we can translate that meaning into a language that people from many different groups can understand, serving as a bridge between the many traditions we straddle.

As we have explored ourselves and our unusual perspective, we have begun to learn that this unique position is one of the reasons we are here. It's why our website is so far-reaching, and also why parts of our teachings are written to appeal to a variety of groups, mixing jargon from Pagans, New Agers, psions, Christian mystics and so forth.

What we are seeking is to develop a spiritual mothertongue -- a language that expresses, clearly and concisely, the basic principles beneath all religious, spiritual, and magickal systems. Through this, we hope to promote tolerance and understanding among the many different expressions of spirituality that can be found on this planet.

Once positive communication has been achieved, we feel that all the different groups and traditions can come together to develop a more complete understanding of the universe and our collective place in it. For we feel each system expresses the truth, but only in part. And only by getting all of the pieces to the jigsaw together will we begin to appreciate the entire picture.

In Pursuit of the Temple

Our beliefs do not exist because they are located in a physical place. Knowledge is not inherent in the bricks of a building or even in the books of a library. It can be stored in a building. It can be recorded in books. But the real answers, the ability to use the knowledge and benefit from it, are in *you*.

You do not need to come spend time at a monastery, temple or church in order to gain understanding of yourself, your nature, and your life. Places like these exist to show you that there are others like you, and to present you the opportunity of gathering with others and sharing your experiences and beliefs.

But the real focus still is you. You are your own monastery, your own temple, your own sacred space. And all the knowledge, all the stillness so crucial to spiritual cultivation are carried within, at your center.

You have all the answers already: you have only forgotten how to listen. Our culture teaches us that we cannot stand on our own. We cannot know something just because we know it; we need authentic degrees and certificates in order to prove our knowledge and understanding to others.

But these things are formalities only. The real authority on your life is *you* -- so seek approval there first.

Trust those little whispers of guidance offered by your inner Self. If you are satisfied with what it tells you, what does it matter what anyone else has to say?

Cults in the Context of Religion

Several years ago, I had the pleasure of lecturing at the local high school on cults and alternative religions. It was a great opportunity, and all the kids and teachers who listened in on the lecture seemed to leave with a new appreciation for tolerance and religious diversity.

I needed an entertaining way to show the students the definition of a cult. So I came up with the anecdote that follows. It's called "The Cult of the Purple Sheep:"

Farmer Bob is a shepherd. He's Christian, and he understand Jesus, the Lord being a Shepherd, too, and all. Well, one day Christ appears to Farmer Bob in the form of a purple sheep. And this sheep walks right up to Farmer Bob and says, "Bob, Christianity's a great religion, but the folks in charge got some things wrong. So I want you to fix those problems. Here's my new message..."

OK, so Farmer Bob has now had a vision -- a revelation as it were. And he goes and preaches his message to his buddies at the local bar. Some of them think he's been out in the sun too long, but a couple of them hear what he has to say and agree with it. These few people start meeting in the barn with Farmer Bob every Tuesday to discuss the message of the purple sheep. Local folks start learning about these meetings, but if you haven't heard the message and agreed with it, then you aren't invited to the meetings. So the locals are left to speculate on what Farmer Bob is really doing in there with all those other farmers, and those sheep...

And by religious definitions, you now have the Cult of the Purple Sheep. They branched off from an established belief system, but with some very different views. They are not big, and they are not widely accepted. They are, in many cases, even feared because their beliefs are not widely known or understood. But there are a few people who believe the message, and these few are pretty loyal and dedicated to their interpretation of the truth.

After some time, Farmer Bob's message gets out to a lot of people. His

little group grows and starts needing more barns to meet in. They start establishing their own rites and rules for doing things that set them more clearly apart as a group unto themselves. They still operate with some of the old structure of Christianity, but they are distinctly doing their own thing. And now they are so big, that when someone talks about Christianity, they have to say, "Well, we've got the Lutherans over there, and the Methodists, the Catholics ... and, um, the

Cult of the Purple Sheep. I know, I know -- it sounds crazy, but some of the things they have to say aren't half bad ... "

So now, the Cult of the Purple Sheep has become a Sect -- a recognized and acknowledged branch of an established religious system. It's still got its roots firmly in its Christian origins, but it is big enough and widespread enough that it has to be acknowledged by those on the outside.

Time passes, and Farmer Bob really starts preaching to people. More and more people join. The system they develop defines their group more and more by their own practices and beliefs, and the influence of Christianity becomes less and less apparent. With a whole lot of believers, a lot of public recognition and acceptance, and rites, organization, and rules that define them as their own group, Farmer Bob's original cult has now become a religion, separate from Christianity. What do they call it?

Baa-baaism -- of course.

* * * *

So after that little anecdote, I asked the class why a cult was bad -- because by all technical definitions, a cult is just an early stage of a newly developing religion. All our notions of "cult" in a bad sense, all our notions of "cult-like activity" -- those are connotations attached to the word through the media, public opinion, and so forth.

After a lively discussion on everything from Wicca to Voodoo, from Waco to Jonestown, we came up with the following criterion for a "dangerous" cult:

1. They take the money of their members, usually trying to make the members who don't donate feel bad for not contributing to the welfare of the group. The authority figures within the group hoard all this money for themselves, spending it on bigger buildings, more decorations, fancier robes, etc.,

2. They discourage members from associating with people who have different beliefs from the group. Members are especially discouraged from marrying or getting into a long-term relationship with anyone who isn't a member. And those outsiders they do get involved with are encouraged to become part of the group before any marriage / relationship will be recognized by the group.

3. They use fear tactics to inspire members to adhere to the group's rules. Members are threatened with terrible

outcomes and made to feel guilty about their actions if they do anything against the rules of the group.

4. Those who question the group's beliefs too much are disciplined and

censured. Questioning the beliefs is severely frowned upon, and members who try to work against this or fight certain beliefs are usually cast out and demonized to the remaining people in the group.

5. Children of the group are indoctrinated from an early age with the group's beliefs, and are discouraged from exploring any belief system save for that of the group.

6. Group leaders are given special privileges. Certain rules that apply to the lay people often do not apply to them. In extreme cases, the group works to allow its leaders to break or avoid the laws of the established culture, or covers up transgressions against the same.

Guess what the class learned? We just described the Catholic Church – as well as just about every other sect of Christianity that exists.

This whole experience simply served to illustrate my point that the cultural definition of a cult and the actual definition of a cult are two entirely different things. According to the media and most lay people, anything which is a cult is bad – it is generally Satanic, oppressive of individual will, and engages in travesties like ritual abuse and animal sacrifice.

However, the textbook definition of a cult is simply a small religion. Christianity was a cult during its nascent days in the Roman Empire, and Wicca was a cult in the early half of the 20th century – though, as Wicca has gained recognition as a religion within the US military and awareness about Wiccans and neo-Paganism continues to grow, I would argue that it is moving out of the "cult" stage and becoming a sect – the next step along the way to becoming a world religion.

It was very satisfying speaking before the students and watching their eyes open up as they were exposed to new ideas. By the end of our animated discussion, even those who were resistant or quietly hostile to the notion of religions other than their own were looking around at the diversity of their peers with a fresh – and much more accepting -- perspective.

Shaping the Spiritus Mundi

Psychologist Carl Jung hit upon a significant and potentially world-altering idea when he described the collective unconscious. In strictly Jungian terms, the collective unconscious is something of a collective racial memory all humans are tied to on an unspoken level. Each race, each person, each culture is influenced by the material contained within this collective memory, and each of these helped to shape the collective over time.

But in my work with magick and mysticism, I have come to understand the collective unconscious in slightly different terms. For me, the collective unconscious exists on the level of pure energy. It has a subtle reality all its own and is a part of the greater *Spiritus Mundi*, the spirit of the world. All humanity influences and is influenced by the collective unconscious. It is the sum total of all their thoughts, dreams, emotions, myths, and nightmares. It is the well of inspiration and creative thought.

The unawakened are unaware of the affect they have upon the collective unconscious. Nor are they aware of how they are in turn affected by it. It helps to define their beliefs, their dreams, their very perception and experience of reality.

Yet it is possible to become consciously aware of our connection to the collective. Thus we can consciously choose what elements will affect us and what will not. In this way, we can shape our individual perceptions of reality and begin to Awaken.

On a more profound level, those who have Awakened to this more profound perception of reality can also consciously influence the collective. We can insert thoughts, ideas, beliefs, and set them adrift on its currents. They will circulate among the masses of humanity, occasionally surfacing in an individual's thoughts, often influencing the behavior, perceptions, and beliefs of the unawakened on a profound yet unspoken level.

In this way, we can shape the reality of others. We can subtly influence thoughts and attitudes on a world-wide scale. Such subtle manipulation is very difficult to master, and it requires an extensive awareness of the collective. Those who seek to influence the world in this way must also be willing to be influenced in turn on an equally profound level. As an active element in a passive world, the collective will surge up and manifest through you. You will become a tool of the *Spiritus Mundi*. It will guide your actions so that you may bring change, destruction, and regeneration where it is needed most.

Archetypes and the Mythic Imagination

Many of us identify strongly with a particular god or goddess, a mythic hero, or perhaps a character out of a book. All of these things appeal to us because we resonate with the archetype which they represent. Archetypes are basically the core players who show up in our myths and our stories, wearing different costumes and sporting different names depending on the culture that gives them expression. In the strictest Jungian sense an archetype is:

> *an inherited idea or mode of thought which is derived from the experience of the race and is present in the unconscious of the individual.*

Put into simpler terms, the Jungian archetype is a symbol that we access through the mythic imagination. It represents an abstract idea or concept and it is often personified. All of our experiences, all our dreams and stories come together in this shared unconscious realm and coalesce into symbols. Archetypes are the characters that populate the mythic imagination, and in a lot of ways they embody fundamental aspects that every human encounters within himself at one point or another.

Some common and immediately recognizable archetypes include the Old Wise Woman and her counterpart, the Hermit. There is the Hero, the Trickster, and the Dark Half (which Jung dubbed "the Shadow"), the Divine Son, the Mother, and sundry others. Many of these archetypes appear and reappear throughout world mythology; they are our gods, our heroes, and our hated villains. They are present in our literature, in our movies, in our art, and even in our dreams.

The archetypes speak to us on the level of myth and symbol. Thus, the dialogue they hold with us goes much deeper than words. The Trickster is still the Trickster, regardless of whether he is called Loki or Raven, Coyote or Hanuman. Across language and across cultures, his message is the same: don't be afraid to look at old things in new ways; don't take the rules so seriously that you allow yourself to become trapped by them.

All gods and goddesses are merely different facets of one of these universal archetypes. This is not to say that their divinity is lacking or invalid. Rather, the archetype is the finite and knowable symbol through which the infinite and unknowable deity manifests. Storm gods the world over are alike in fundamental ways. Zeus, Thor, Baal, and Yahweh are all virile and have potent tempers. Each is a personification of how early humans viewed the storm: inimical, awe-inspiring, and driven by a passionate sentience.

A good corollary for the relation between archetype and divinity can be found in the Hebrew mystical tradition. In this system, divinity is so vast, so unknowable, that one cannot even utter its name. Yet that vastly unknowable deity makes itself manifest through smaller and smaller emanations. These emanations, called Sephiroth (which means, literally "sapphires" or "jewels"), are aspects of the divinity, filtering down through the cosmos like light filtering through clouds. The closer they get to humanity, the more limited and human they become. However, there is a reflexive quality to this process of emanation, for the more limited and human the Sephiroth become, the easier it is for us to contain and comprehend them.

Archetypes are the equivalent of these emanations. They embody some aspect of the limitless divine in a finite persona that we can better relate to. When we give an archetype a name, such as Odin, Brighid, Mary, or Mithras, we then draw it down even further, bringing it closer to our human, personal level so that we may comprehend its nature with our finite, human minds. The ultimate comprehension is identification, when the lines between the knower and that which is known blur and merge.

Such anthropomorphic gods and goddesses are necessarily limited and human in aspect; that is how we can identify with them. People do not relate to Jesus simply because he was the Son of God. People relate to him because he was compassionate, he ate and drank with his friends, and he had moments of weakness and doubt. In short, he was human. Devout Christians are expected to be like Jesus, to identify themselves with him everyday. In Christian mysticism, this goes beyond merely living like Jesus to achieving a perfect union with the Christ within. The goal of Christianity is to become the Christ – essentially, assume the archetype.

This is a very important yet difficult concept. Archetypes do not simply express the divinity around us. Our connection to archetypes really comes from inside of us. The archetype becomes the expression of the divinity that each of us carries within our soul. Within or without, archetypes are the bridges between human and the divine, putting the infinite into a shape and symbol that our finite minds can comprehend.

Our internal language is the language of symbol, and this internal symbol-system is unique to each and every individual. As each of our symbol-systems vary widely, so too are there wide variations in the faces of divinity with which we can relate. Thus, while Loki may appeal to one person as the best expression of the divinity within himself, Hathor may appeal to another and Jesus Christ to yet another. In some cases, one single archetype will not suffice to embody the complexity of that individual's spirit, and thus many gods and goddesses are called upon to do the job. In some cases, the archetype does not even take the form of a recognizable god, but can be a personality drawn from myth or from literature – anything that strongly resonates with the characteristics which that individual person relates to within their Self and in the divine.

What forms these archetypes take or how many each person relates to does not matter. The names and the faces might change, but the truth beyond the godform is still the same. Harnessing this internal god is what empowers an individual and gives him access to abilities commonly attributed to the divine: it allows him to see the hidden aspects of reality, to change the world with just his will, to reach upward, beyond his ordinary human limitations to the awareness of the divine. When someone is in touch with their particular archetype, this is union in a mystical sense. It is an apotheosis, and it is this connection that people strive toward in all mystical practices and religious rites.

Many people seek to project their archetype outside of themselves, and thus make it into a God to be worshipped, a

God that is prayed to, appeased, and supplicated. But this does not have to be the case. The divinity within is the same as the divinity without. And in many ways, it is much more empowering to accept the god that lies within. We are all divine, and if we understand enough of ourselves and the universe around us, then we can harness that divinity through our particular archetype and transcend the limits of ordinary existence. Our archetype becomes nothing less than the face we assume when we are informed and empowered by the divinity, which is ultimately is a fundamental part of us.

Thou art God, thou art Goddess. The same light is shining everywhere. The only difference is the filter we let it shine through.

Blurring the Lines

There is a certain bias in the occult community concerning works of fantasy. I understand it, for I have it, too. When someone speaks to me of an idea or concept, no matter how potentially valid, if it turns out that their source of inspiration was a novel, a movie, a game -- then I am less inclined to listen to anything else they have to say.

And yet, as my career has taken me deeper into the publishing industry, I've learned a few things. These things were revelatory at first, although I suppose they really shouldn't have surprised me. But then, our culture as a whole has another ingrained bias, and that is to view someone who has done something such as write a book or a movie or put out a CD as Someone Official.

Anyone who has become published often loses their existence as ordinary people like you and me. Instead, they are elevated to being a Concept. When we learn their name by reading it on the spine of a book or even in the credits of a movie, we subsequently tend to perceive them as being somehow different from us – they can't possibly share the same hopes and dreams and flaws as lowly ordinary humanity. They are Important People who live in big houses and do great things.

But I've met writers now and artists, musicians, even movie-makers. And they're just like you and me. They have hopes and fears and dreams. They read many of the same books that we do, they watch the same shows. They can be fans of someone else's work, and they certainly have their own ideas and beliefs, developed, much like ours, through the sum of their culture, education, and experiences.

Most importantly, they're people whose art imitates their life, who can't help but sneak in little inside jokes that only their circle of friends might perceive, who write characters and stories only thinly disguised from the things in their lives that inspired them. Their creative efforts are inevitably influenced by their religious, political, and personal beliefs. And almost always, they draw their inspiration from what they live, what they know, spinning it into something everyone else will dare believe.

The revelation for me was that many of these people -- especially the ones who create in the genres that we crave -- are just like us -- they share our convictions and our beliefs. This is of course to a greater and lesser extent for each, and some of them are open about their influence from magick and the occult (consider Tori Amos and the spirits and faeries she communes with for inspiration with her songs), while others are using a creative medium to express ideas that they might not be able to publish in a non-fiction work (do you have any idea how many thirty and forty-something fiction writers in the SF/Fantasy genres are Pagans or occultists and simply cannot be open about this fact because of publicity & marketing concerns?). But to think that their work does not often seek to express some truth they hold dear is to be deceived.

I forget who said it exactly, but some pundit declared that all novelists write stories to proclaim through the veil of fiction those beliefs they are afraid to proclaim publicly. And it's quite true. And that's to say nothing of those who write both fiction and non-fiction, and simply use their fiction as an entertaining vehicle to pass on beliefs.

Consider Crowley's book, *Moon Child.* This is a novel penned by the author of *Magick Without Tears.* It is most definitely a work of fiction, but its author also wrote it with the intention of expressing the laws and theories behind a process that he believed was possible: the creation of a magickal child. Dion Fortune, similarly, wrote novels with the intention of demonstrating her lifestyle, practices, and beliefs through a fictional medium.

My point in this rambling is that there are many vehicles for truth to be carried in, and stories are often more accessible to beginners than heavy, jargon-laden treatises. I would not go so far as to suggest that someone should take everything written about in fantasy as thinly veiled fact, or live a game as if it were reality -- but I am saying that, if you look in the right places, you'll be surprised by the very valid insights you might see. Stories offer more than mere diversion -- many of them are our new myths. I don't think it's wrong to admit this fact and explore the things that they have to teach.

Demons, Cleansings, and Faith

Use the word demon around just about anyone, and its likely to conjure images of a Judeo-Christian Heaven and Hell, thoroughly dualistic and founded upon judgment, damnation, and original sin. And yet the notion of demons – non-human spirits of chaos and destruction that behave malevolently toward humanity – is older than both the Christian and the Jewish faith. Christianity got both its angelology and its demonology from the Jews, and the Jews in their turn inherited much of their views on these spirits from the Babylonians. The Babylonians, in their stead, derived most of their ideas from the Sumerians, and the Sumerian culture is so old that it would be hard to say what society their beliefs were derived from, as conventional archaeology refuses to accept a civilization that predated theirs.

But the concept of demons is an old one, and a belief in these types of spirits does not have to rely upon a strictly Judeo-Christian worldview. As a Pagan, I have encountered spirits that I can only describe as demonic. They are rare, and I am very, very cautious about giving a spirit that descriptor. In my opinion, there are many types of spirits out there, and because of our largely Judeo-Christian cultural bias, too many people are far too quick to label something a demon simply because it seems a little "dark." Spirits that truly earn the term demons are rare, but from my point of view, I think both me & a Catholic can agree that there are some spirits out there that are really negative, non-human, and seem to love nothing more than messing with people in a nasty and malicious fashion. I might not believe in the same sort of Heaven and Hell as a Catholic, but I can certainly agree that such a spirit fits the common understanding of what a demon's supposed to be.

If a family thinks the spirit plaguing them is a demon, and I really disagree with this assessment, I might try to point out that there are a lot of different type of spirits out there, tons of non-human entities, and many things that might seem like demons because they are mean and aggressive. But in the end, if they can only see the spirit as a demon because that's the framework their beliefs allow them to have, then I work within that framework. When it comes to resolving the haunting for a family in order to make them feel safe in their space, what they believe is far more important than what I believe. And I think this is an important approach to consider for any person – clergy or otherwise – who finds themselves in a position to advise or assist others in the paranormal realm. As much as many modern-day ghost-hunters may try to obtain irrefutable proof of the existence of ghosts through an array of technological and pseudo-scientific gadgetry, the fact of the matter is that supernatural experiences are still the province of belief rather than fact. Paranormal solutions for people should then speak in the language of belief, with an emphasis on the belief system and worldview of the individuals who feel victimized by their experiences.

Again, as Pagan clergy, I think I'm especially suited to this sort of mental/spiritual flexibility. Pagans don't have one Scripture that they follow. Most don't even follow the same gods. (the best way to grasp this is to think of denominations of Christians, only Christ might be called Biff in one and Bob in another and Mary Sue in a third). When I do a wedding or house blessing or whatever, the first thing I usually do is to learn the shape of the person's faith: what god or goddess that person follows, the tradition of Paganism that they adhere to, etc.,

From my own personal faith, all divinities are faces of the Divine -- since the Divine is infinite and we are finite, we can only ever see the Divine in bits and pieces anyway. It's like staring at a huge, faceted jewel, where I see a part of it from where I'm standing, and you see a part of it from where you're standing. While we each see vastly different things, in the end, we're looking at the same jewel. So it doesn't bother me to work with a person's faith. I value the faith itself, and I think it's one of our greatest powers. And it's important to encourage people to find that faith in themselves by whatever road or symbols will best lead them there.

Shamanism: Transcending the Limits of Reality

Shamanism is, in the loosest sense, a mystical technique utilized to gain access to the realm of spirits. It has been characterized as many things, including a "technique of ecstasy" by Mircea Eliade (Eliade, 4), a "method rather than a religion" by Michael Harner (Doore, 1992: 5), and "a religio-magical complex" by Ake Hultkrantz (Hultkrantz, 1988: 36). In the past, anthropologists have studied it with a certain amount of scholarly detachment, regarding it as something of a curiosity isolated to "primitive religions" (Eliade, 7). However there has been a recent revival in the West's interest in shamanism. With anthropologist Michael Harner and British mystic Neville Drury at the forefront, more and more Western thinkers have begun to advocate shamanism as a personal mystical practice assimilable into the modern mystical movement. As such, it is coming to be included in such imported mystical practices as yoga, Zen Buddhism, and Tantric meditation.

Of course, before we define shamanism as a mystical technique, it would be helpful to put forth a definition of what we mean by the term “mystical”. Many writers who address issues of religion and religious experience often make distinctions between religious officials such as priests and monks, devotees, lay persons, and "mystics," yet the distinctions between these categories, especially that between the priest, the religious devotee and the mystic, are ambiguous at best. In the case of St. John of the Cross or St. Theresa of Avila, it is clear that clerics can be mystics, but in the case of Siddartha who was a prince of the warrior class before he became the Buddha, we see that a mystic does not necessarily have to be a priest. Further, many famous religious thinkers whose works have served as the foundation of religious movements, may not fall into the category of mystic. Certainly St. Augustine was a great thinker, but did his words arise from the same sort of intense, immediate visionary experiences as the words of St. Theresa of Avila?

Surveying the reports of mystics and mystical experiences from all the various cultures, times, and religions that have flickered across the face of this earth, we seem to see a kind of pattern forming, but it is of a negative image. It only tells us what mystical experience is not: it is not limited to the priestly class; it is not limited to scholars of religion nor to staunch devotees of a particular religion; it is not limited to the social, economical, or even the intellectual elite; it is not even limited to a particular religion, but appears equally in nearly every religion across the globe.

Individual reports of an intense, ineffable, enlightening experience, while not common, are certainly a phenomenon shared by all religious systems. While a particular god or a particular creed may not be universal, religious numinosa apparently is. And in every instance, the individual, now a mystic because he was touched by that ineffable but inarguable mystical experience, is somehow significantly and profoundly changed by that experience. His attitude toward life is changed, and he takes joy and suffering with equal acceptance and equal poise. His attitude toward death is likewise changed; he no longer fears what lies beyond and, while he does not attempt to hasten his own end, when death does come, he slips into its arms as if it were a gentle mother. Further, he claims to have a better understanding of the nature and purpose of the universe because he has glimpsed first hand the divine force that guides that universe.

The fundamental claim of a mystic is that he senses and at least partially comprehends those things such as spirits, angels, and even gods, which lie outside the realm of ordinary human experience. While in the Qabbalistic system, the mystic attempts to reach only the throne of God, maintaining that it is impossible for a mere mortal to ever touch God himself, many mystics have claimed to have a direct, unmediated experience of the deity. Their mystical experience, as in the case of St. Theresa of Avila, is described as one of union. St. Theresa as well as St. John of the Cross described this union as a marriage, and in Tantric Buddhism, the union is represented even more graphically as actual coitus between the deity and his consort.

The mystic is the elite member of a religious system, standing at the pinnacle of religious experience. Certainly the common lay persons cannot claim the same direct experience as the mystic. Even the priests and highest officials of a religion who serve as the mouthpiece of the deity cannot claim to have been graced with such an immediate experience of the divine. However, in most cases, the mystic's elite status does not earn him a privileged seat at the head of a religious movement; quite the contrary, he is often met with suspicion from the other members of his and other religions. Ruling officials may declare him a heretic; he may be imprisoned or even put to death for what he claims to have experienced; his words may simply be ignored as the ravings of a madman or a fraud. Direct experience of the divine is no little thing; religions are made and destroyed by those claiming such experience. And since such experience is so rare, it may take a very long time for other members of a religion to credit or even acknowledge the validity of a mystic's experience.

We have said quite a bit of mystics, but as far as mysticism and mystical experience go, we are still working mostly off of a negative image. So what is mystical experience? There are many single words that come up in descriptions of such an experience: ineffable; transformative; intense; immediate; unmediated. None of these by itself adequately describes the experience, but it captures some small part of what we term "mystical experience." For the purposes of this study, we will be working from as simplified a definition of mystical experience as possible. A mystical experience can be defined as an intense, transformative, and often visionary experience during which the individual achieves a sense of union with a divine source, whether that source be divine love, divine wisdom, or the deity itself. Therefore, mysticism is any technique of achieving such an experience. Further, though mystical practices are not limited to any single religious system nor any particular social, economic, or intellectual class, they do seem to be limited to the spiritual elite of all systems.

Shamanism, then, may be considered one of the many techniques of achieving mystical experience. The practitioner of shamanism, called a shaman, "specializes in a trance during which his soul is believed to leave his body and ascend to the sky or descend to the underworld" (Eliade, 5). The word "shaman" comes from a Tungus (Siberian) term, and in the strictest anthropological sense is limited to the mystical techniques particular to that region. But it is misleading to relegate the practice of what is currently understood as shamanism to any one specific area; shamanic techniques have been employed by people around the world, from Siberia to Central America, Australia, Tibet, and Celtic Great Britain (Noll, 1987: 47).

The role of the shaman is many-faceted. In certain capacities, he is an ecstatic, a mystic, a healer, and even a poet. He may participate in some of the ritual functions of priest or medicine man. In his ability to commune with spirits, he may be compared to a medium or visionary, and his divinatory powers may mark him as a magician. Yet the office of shaman is unique and distinct from all of these because the shaman performs all these functions through a method which is unique to him alone. Master of the shamanic journey, the shaman exists within two realities, freely passing back and forth between them as he wills.

In any study of the subject, it is important to acknowledge that the practice of shamanism is as varied as it is widespread. The dress, the ritual tools, and all other such particulars of the shaman vary greatly from culture to culture. It would be next to impossible to address each particular sort of shamanism within the limited scope of a study such as this. Several detailed, cross-cultural analyses have been made on the subject, most notably those of Eliade and Kalweit. It is through a synthesis of the material presented in such studies that I have attempted to arrive at a general definition of "shamanism." In this study, we shall examine the most widespread beliefs and techniques that seem to form the common element of shamanism and then address how those techniques can be used as a method of achieving mystical experience.

The Shaman and Reality

Many modern studies of religious experience and especially those of mystical experience are shallow, biased, and unfair to their subject matter. Such studies begin in the spirit of universal acceptance, proposing to analyze foreign systems of thought in order to gain better understanding of a potentially valid world-view. However, through the very analysis of those systems, these studies end up glorifying Western science and reason while at the same time discrediting and invalidating the "primitive" and "unsophisticated" systems which are ultimately seen as little more than developmental stages societies must endure in the process of achieving the highest form of human thought: reason. In such logicocentric studies, mystics such as the shaman and medicine man are portrayed as charlatans at best and as deluded fools at worst. If a culture so much as dares to believe in spirits, they are labeled superstitious and primitively animistic.

Of course, coming from a culture that clings to its monistic materialist paradigm, it is difficult for us to see the shaman as anything more than a superstitious primitive or a madman. Certainly in our culture those who don't grow out of the stage of having imaginary friends and speaking to inanimate objects are often taken in for counseling. Their differences are viewed as deviant; because their actions go against the popular beliefs of the culture (i.e. there are no such thing as invisible friends; animals and plants are not sentient beings and cannot speak or be spoken to in any serious manner), such individuals are looked upon as somehow broken and in need of being repaired. The role and function of the shaman and to a certain extent even that of the priest has been erased from our culture. We have no way of responding to people who maintain a belief in things we cannot see except to treat such people as ill and attempt to cure them.

It is a symptom of the limitations of our culture's current *Weltenshauung* that anything that does not conform wholly to our materialist, reductionist reality is necessarily considered a deviation. Our culture's concept of the nature of the universe is so narrow that it cannot even allow for the possibility that such experiences may be valid and are simply not accounted for in our limited view of the universe. The common method of addressing such deviancies is automatically to assume that they are invalid and therefore in need of correction. Whether through medication or intensive therapy, any view that does not fit Western science's reductionist view of the universe is discredited and destroyed. The individual must be cured of his pathologically wrong way of thinking before he can assume a normal, healthy existence within society, but he especially must be cured before that society can feel comfortable having him in it once more.

In order to discuss shamanism and mystical experience as fairly as possible, we must take a phenomenological approach and try to abandon our assumptions of what is possible and what is real. There is no context for shamanic experience within the confines of a materialist mindset; the shamanic experience is predicated on a dualistic vision of reality. From a shaman's perspective, the experiential world contains non-physical and supra-physical levels in addition to the more familiar and tangible physical levels of reality. To judge a shaman's approach to reality in terms of illusion or mental illness is to negate the validity of a belief system that is merely different from our own.

Shamanic Consciousness

The practice of shamanism is typified by the shaman's ability to enter an altered state of consciousness at will. This altered state is often termed the "shamanic trance," but the use of the word trance in this context can be misleading. When one enters a trance, one enters an altered state of consciousness, but the general use of "falling into" a trance implies a loss of control over one's faculties. The shaman generally experiences no such loss of control. Much of a shaman's training is devoted to teaching him this crucial control. Mediums or the possessed who enter trance-states have little to no control over themselves throughout the duration of the trance and they further can only rarely recall anything they said or did while under the influence of the spirits. The shaman, on the other hand, retains complete awareness and control of his faculties during the trance-state (Eliade, 5 -- 6).

Thus shamanic trance is distinct from other trances in several ways. Primary among these, of course, is the matter of volition. Unlike the trances of mediums or other individuals who become possessed by spirits, the shaman willfully enters the trance-state and embarks upon a spiritual journey during which he is in control. Further, the shaman retains a conscious memory of the events which take place during this journey

(Noll, 1983: 444 -- 445). In order to distinguish between the trance-states of mediums or the possessed and the trance-states particular to shamans, anthropologist Michael Harner coined the term Shamanic State of Consciousness, henceforth abbreviated as SSC (Harner, 1990: xix). The term SSC implies that an altered state of consciousness is engaged by the shaman while at the same time distinguishing that state from other altered states by marking it as uniquely shamanic.

The SSC has been characterized as an "ecstasy," "trance," or "vision" (Noll, 1987: 49). It is an intense experience of mental imagery which "can become so vivid that it can block out the awareness of normal visual perception" (Noll, 1987: 49). It has been likened to the experience of lucid dreaming. In the shamanic practice of the Australian Unambal, the interior geography to which the shaman travels in the SSC is referred to as the "dreamtime" (*Lalai*), further suggesting its similarity to a controlled dream state (Kalweit, 196). However, while the SSC may be compared to a controlled dream state in order to convey a sense of the vividness of its imagery, it is important to distinguish it from a dream.

When dreaming, one is generally not in control of the events in the dream and further, those events are not perceived as being capable of having an impact upon the dreamer himself or his waking reality. The SSC however is seen as having a unique reality of its own. Those things which occur to the shaman within the confines of the SSC are perceived as having an impact upon him and his waking reality (Harner, 1990: 20 -- 21). Things done by the shaman in the SSC are perceived as having in reality been done; the memories of the SSC are considered as valid as any of the shaman's waking memories. Indeed, they may hold an even greater validity because the remembered events took place within a sacred geography. Because of this, they have potentially profound affects upon both waking reality and the reality of the SSC.

The ontological reality of events in the SSC hinges upon a belief in the connection between spirit and matter. Those things that occur within the SSC are believed to occur upon a spiritual level. This level is separate from and yet intricately connected to the material realm of ordinary reality. Entities and objects from material reality have reflections, as it were, in spiritual reality, just as entities and objects in the spiritual realm can have reflections in material reality. When a shaman enters the SSC, he in effect crosses over to the spiritual realm and can thus interact with it and its inhabitants. By influencing objects, entities, and events within this spiritual realm, the shaman hopes to somehow affect those things connected to these spiritual realities within the ordinary material realm. At its most basic, this can be seen as a kind of sympathetic magic; if the shaman can remove the source of an illness from his patient on the spiritual level, he then increases his chances of removing that illness from him on the physical, material level. However, this is a gross over-simplification of the process and it diminishes the importance of the interconnectedness of spirit and matter perceived by the shaman. To the shaman, illness is not merely physical in nature but nor is it merely spiritual. Illness results from a complex interaction of both physical and spiritual afflictions, and in order to cure his patient, the shaman must treat the illness in both realities.

It is a common mistake of Westerners to immediately dismiss the reality of the SSC as simple fantasy on the basis that it takes place "all in one's head." At best, it is accepted as therapeutic "guided imagery" (Drury, 46), but as such it is still relegated to the realm of fantasy, albeit useful fantasy. It is crucial to understand that for the shaman the SSC goes much deeper than mere mental imagery. It has a reality of its own, and this reality is distinct from but of no less importance than ordinary waking reality (Kalweit, 11). From this, it is probably clear that the shaman's view of reality does not conform to what the West in general has come to accept as reality. But in order to understand shamanism, one must first see through a shaman's eyes, a trick which requires a particular sort of double-vision.

This brings us to a point of contention between proponents of shamanism and certain thinkers in the West. The dream-like and hallucinatory characteristics of the shaman's journey, combined with the initiatory illness often characteristic of the shaman's call, have led several Western thinkers to argue that shamanism is no more than a form of schizophrenia that was given an acceptable social function by primitive societies that did not know how else to deal with mental illness (Noll, 1983: 446 -- 447). Certainly, from the traditional Western standpoint of monistic materialism, it is easier to accept the shamanic journey as purely a vision or hallucination rather than a legitimate spiritual experience.

The monistic materialist paradigm that serves as the foundation of so much of Western thought, particularly in the sciences, disavows the possibility of man's existence as a dual being composed of both a material and a spiritual existence. Limited in their studies of reality to the mere physical material of man and his universe, such Western thinkers would prefer to limit their definition of reality to those things which readily submit themselves to their traditional methods of inquiry and verification. Such thinkers are very reluctant to admit that those methods may be limited in their ability to scrutinize, categorize, and define the whole of reality. Some are openly hostile to alternate views of reality which are seen to imply that their monistic materialism is an inadequate approach to the whole nature of reality.

Because of this persistent faith in their world-view, many Western scientists as well as the lay persons subsequently influenced by their mode of thinking blind themselves even to the possibility of a spiritual as well as a physical reality. This is not the case with the shaman. Shamanism presupposes a reality which has both a spiritual as well as a material existence. As stated previously, as far as the shaman is concerned, the journey and everything that is encountered along the way is real. However, our understanding of what is "real" must be qualified in regards to the distinction between what Carlos Casteneda's Yaqui teacher Don Juan termed "ordinary reality" and "nonordinary reality" (Harner, 1990: xix).

Ordinary reality is that reality in which man finds himself on a daily basis, the reality where he works and eats and interacts with other men. In ordinary reality one can speak of mythological beasts that are imagined but are not real. One understands that there are certain rules to existence in ordinary reality: animals don't talk, people can't fly, and spirits do not just come down out of the clouds, sit down on a rock, and engage in conversation with the living. Nonordinary reality, on the other hand, is the reality at work in dreams, visions, and the SSC. In nonordinary reality one cannot think of mythological beasts as imaginary and unreal; dragons and griffons are as likely to appear in non-ordinary reality as are rabbits or deer. Unlike ordinary reality, in nonordinary reality people can fly, animals do talk, and spirits as well as animals, gods, and demons are entirely likely to come down out of the sky or up from the ground to engage one in conversation. Like ordinary reality, nonordinary reality functions off a certain set of rules. In ordinary reality, the rules can be studied and learned through the application of science. In nonordinary reality, it is the shaman or the magician and not the scientist who is equipped to study and understand the laws of the universe.

The shaman is unique among men because he has been gifted with a sort of double-vision. Through his initiation, he has undergone the shamanic "enlightenment" (Harner, 1990: 22 -- 24); he can see with his "strong eye" (Noll, 1987: 50). With this unique vision, the shaman is aware of and able to perceive at will both ordinary and nonordinary reality. For him, it becomes irrelevant to make a distinction between "real" and "not-real." The only distinction is between ordinary reality and nonordinary reality. The shaman is aware of both at once and therefore, for him, the rules on what is real and possible shift depending upon how he "looks" at things.

His ability to distinguish between the two states of reality separates the shaman from the schizophrenic. Shamanism is further distinguished from an abnormal psychological state by that which defines the shamanic technique of ecstasy: control. In terms of the spirit-realm, the shaman acts; he is not acted upon. The shaman controls the spirits in that he can speak to them, bargain with them, and drive them away if they become threatening and the need to do so arises (Noll, 1987: 55). Further, he does not simply slip into the SSC randomly; he chooses where and when he will embark upon the shamanic journey. In this matter more than all others, he is in control, and it is his control of this spiritual journey that distinguishes him as a shaman.

First Steps of the Journey

When he enters SSC, the shaman leaves his physical body behind and travels in his shaman's body or spirit body (Drury, 9 -- 10). Typically, he then goes to a gateway. This may be a tree he must climb, a hole he must crawl down, or even a pool of water into which he dives (Harner, 1990: 25 -- 30). Usually, this gateway has been shown to him by another shaman or by a guiding spirit. The shaman passes through the gateway and travels through a tunnel which opens up onto the upper or lower world (Harner, 1990: 29 -- 30). Once there, he interacts with the creatures of the other realms, conversing with gods, demons, spirits, and animals. These may give him gifts, often in the forms of pebbles, darts, or feathers. It is typical of the shaman that, upon accepting the gift, he somehow makes it a part of his body, either by swallowing it or inserting it directly into his flesh. In the latter case, the flesh will magically close up around the object and it will travel painlessly to a place of power in the shaman's body, such as his liver or in the hollow of his chest. Each gift adds to the shaman's power, and they remain lodged inside his shaman body so they will always be at hand when he needs them (Harner, 1990: 17).

The shaman further befriends many greater and lesser spirits, and these become his guides and assistants in both the spiritual realm and the realm of men. They help him heal the sick, drive away malevolent forces, and find his way through the dreamtime. Particularly potent spirit-helpers take the form of animal spirits known as "power animals" (Harner, 1990: 58). Rather like individual embodiments of a mythological animal archetype, they can appear in animal, human, or theriomorphic form. They not only assist the shaman but also contribute their own abilities to his:

> When possessed by a shaman, the power animal acts as an alter-ego, imparting to the shaman the power of transformation . . .
>
> (Harner, 1990: 59)

The spirits may also act as teachers to the shaman, revealing to him the secrets of the dreamtime, teaching him how to use his shamanic vision, and instructing him in the art of healing. Spirit teachers are so common that most shamans receive little formal training after their initiation; the rest of their schooling is left to what mentors they may encounter upon their further journeys into the dreamtime (Harner, 1988: 14). Many shamans even receive their initiation from some sort of spirit guide who leads the initiate "through the imaginal 'lower world' in order to learn the arcane arts of shamanism" (Noll, 1987: 53).

These spirit mentors often take the form of ancestors who were once shamans themselves. They choose the shaman-to-be from early childhood, sometimes even from birth, often marking him with something which sets him apart from the rest of the members of his community. Perhaps because one of the shaman's main functions is that of healer, this distinguishing factor is often associated with illness, suggesting that a true healer cannot deal with illness and pain unless he has experienced it in himself. It may be a physical deformity or it may be an illness that took the chosen shaman to the brink of death where he had an experience which foreshadowed his shamanic initiation and subsequent journeys into the underworld. It may even be a sort of mental signature which sets the shaman-to-be apart from his peers as sharply as any overt physical deformity. He may have the ability to perceive and speak with spirits long before his formal training begins. He may experience visions, and in some cases, he may even enjoy the contact of the spirit who is to be his mentor long before he reaches the age at which he is to be initiated as a shaman.

The Shaman’s Initiation

The shaman's initiation is often violent and traumatic. The spirits may begin by sending him dreams of things to come, or he may become possessed by a spirit and be forced to master it (Krippner, 126). In many cases, the first "journey" occurs spontaneously and is not actively sought after by the initiate. Since the shaman does not yet know how to go to the spirits or is unwilling to do so, the spirits come to the shaman and lift him right out of his reality. This is how they choose him to become a shaman (Kalweit, 106 -- 107).

Often the shaman's initiation is accompanied by a severe physical illness (Harner, 1988: 13). He will come near the point of death but then undergo a sudden recovery. He may even believe that he has died; funeral preparations may be underway as he wakes up, miraculously cured. This death and figurative rebirth marks him as a potential shaman. Having been healed of his illness, it is believed that he gains the ability to heal others. He becomes the "wounded healer" (Achterberg, 115), one who has undergone a personal crisis, survived it, and is able to use the knowledge he gained through that survival to assist others in their own crises (Achterberg, 117).

Symbolically, the initiate dies and is resurrected by the spirits that have chosen to held and guide him (Kalweit, 9 -- 10). As Kalweit puts it, "The simplest and most drastic way to change someone's state of consciousness is to kill him or bring him close to death" (Kalweit, 8). Such an experience separates the potential shaman from the rest of the community:

> Social isolation, a plague of odd thoughts,
> and the likelihood of personality alteration
> all characterize the fledgeling shaman's experience . . .
> Shamans-to-be encounter raw glimpses of
> something numinous and demanding, some threat
> or promise in their own landscape of dreams.

(Schmidt, 64)

The shaman-to-be is thrust into a liminal existence. The period of his initiation "strips the shaman of all his social and mental habits as well as his religious and philosophical ideas" (Kalweit, 95). He is literally born over again, thrust suddenly, naked and defenseless, into a world that has become unfamiliar to him.

The death and rebirth motif is a crucial part of shamanic initiation. Not only does the shaman undergo a symbolic physical death; he often undergoes a very elaborate and gruesome death in the SSC. His soul is abducted by the spirits which seek to initiate him as a shaman. Typically they dismember him, stripping off his flesh and grilling it over a fire. The spirits then divide his flesh up among themselves and eat it; if there is not enough flesh for all of the spirits to have some, the shaman will not be able to cure all illnesses (Kalweit, 108). When there is nothing left of him but a skeleton, the spirits take him apart and rearrange his bones in such a way as to give him superhuman powers (Kalweit, 95). Or the shaman may be devoured by an animal mother and reborn as an animal; he is destroyed and then reformed within her and his new animal-self then becomes one of his power animals (Kalweit, 107).

The initiate's death and rebirth is a metaphor for his change from an ordinary person to a shaman. It is during this change that the spirits bestow upon him his powers as a shaman. By being torn apart and devoured piece by piece by the spirits, he gains his abilities as a healer. When he is put back together, stones or sacred objects are often inserted into his body to make him invulnerable and to protect him from evil spirits (Kalweit, 108). It is also during this torturous initiation that the shaman usually receives his "shamanic enlightenment," a kind of clairvoyance which allows him to see with his eyes closed, enabling him to perceive both the world of men and the world of spirits (Noll, 1987: 50). This enlightenment or illumination is characterized as

> a light inside his head, within the brain, [which enables him to] perceive things and coming events which are hidden from others . . . Nothing is hidden from him any longer. He can also discover stolen souls that are kept concealed in far, strange lands or have been taken to the land of the dead.

(Kalweit, 203)

From the moment of his call throughout the duration of his initiation, the shaman exists in a liminal state. The world around him is rearranged; everything which he previously held to be "true and natural" is transformed (Schmidt, 65). His perception, his consciousness, even his body is torn asunder and reconstructed in a subtly different fashion. This death and rebirth makes the shaman "twice-born" (Kalweit, 1). Having undergone a personal crisis, he returns capable of assisting others through their crises. Having endured illness and pain, he returns with the ability to heal. Having experienced death, he is now able to help others die, escorting their souls to the land of the dead from which he has returned.

The Functions of the Shaman

The shaman's position within his community is unique. He is like the priest in that he deals with spirits and has contact with "higher powers." During important rituals, the priest officiates, but the shaman is expected to be present as well. It is the shaman's duty to maintain an auspicious atmosphere for the ritual, keeping malevolent spirits from interfering with the proceedings. If a sacrifice is involved, the priest performs the sacrifice while the shaman soothes the spirit of the sacrificed animal, asking its blessing and forgiveness, then, in his role of psychopomp, escorting its spirit down to the realm of the dead.

The shaman rarely has any place in the ritual itself, however, for ritual is the domain of the priest. Similarly, the priest could not perform the shaman's role in the proceedings because his domain is doctrine and ritual; he rarely if ever is expected to have unmediated contact with spirits or gods, and he is certainly never expected to embark upon the visionary, otherworldly journey unique to the shaman. The priest's function is far more formal than ecstatic and it is distinctly locked within the limits of ordinary reality. The priest transcends those limits only rarely: he may receive messages and insight from his deities in the form of visions, but only the shaman can willfully move between the reality of the ritual and the non-ordinary reality of the vision.

The shaman is a healer, a prognosticator, a dealer with spirits, but all of these functions are carried out through the shamanic journey. He is initiated as a shaman through such a journey and all of his subsequent powers and gifts are received within the context of the journey. It is the core of his function; it is the shaman's control over the SSC and his subsequent harnessing of the shamanic journey which distinguishes him from ordinary healers, magicians, and holy men (Eliade, 5).

The shamanic journey may be undertaken for several different reasons. Most frequently, the shaman enters the SSC in order to fulfill his role as both spiritual and physical healer in the community. In the shamanic system, illness may be caused by a "loss of power" or a "loss of soul." The lost power often takes the form of a power animal which the shaman must chase down in the SSC and return to its rightful owner (Harner, 1990: 69). Other forms of illness are brought about by "power intrusions" (Harner, 1990: 115), the presence of foreign objects in the body. These objects are of a spiritual nature and are only visible to the eyes of the shaman that can see both ordinary and nonordinary reality. The shaman enters the SSC and looks inside his patient, searching for those things that do not belong. Once he sees them, he removes them by sucking them out (Harner, 1990: 116). Once again, these two typically shamanic techniques of healing demonstrate how intrinsic the belief in the interconnectedness of spirit and matter is to the shamanic system.

The shaman also serves in the capacity of psychopomp. In this function, he enters the SSC in order to escort the souls of the dead safely to the realm of the underworld, thus ensuring that they will rest peacefully and not bother the living relatives they left behind (Eliade, 182). As Freud pointed out in his *Totem and Taboo*, the lingering presence of the spirits of the dead is greatly feared by "primitive" societies the world round. While the physical existence of the dead is given a proper and necessary sense of closure through funerary rituals, it is up to the shaman to extend that sense of closure beyond the mere physical, insuring that spirit as well as body is laid to rest.

The shaman does much of his dealings with the dead, resembling in this respect the necromancer of the west. He sometimes receives instruction from former shamans or powerful ancestors that have passed beyond life. He may also enter the SSC in order to converse with the dead, receiving knowledge about the weather, the whereabouts of lost items, or secret teachings and revelations from them. In this he not only resembles the traditional necromancer but also the *palos* of Santeria, who summons spirits of the dead for many of the same functions, though the shaman, unlike the *palos* very rarely binds such spirits in order to keep them as servants.

Knowledge, on subjects from the weather to the movement of the herds, is often a goal of the shamanic journey; as prognosticator, the shaman enters the SSC in order to perceive those things hidden from men in ordinary reality. Or he may seek out creatures of power, elemental spirits and nature deities, in order to learn from them or to gain some spiritual favor (Drury, 25 -- 26).

From these applications of the shamanic journey, it is clear that the role of the shaman is a communal one. He is selected by the spirits to represent his people in the sacred geography of the dreamtime. When the nonordinary reality with which he is so familiar somehow infringes upon the ordinary reality of his community, it is the shaman's responsibility to set things right. As such, he is the mediator of the cosmos, and it is up to him to look both ways for those who cannot.

Envisioning the Active Feminine

In myth, we most often see woman portrayed as the archetypal Mother, the nurturer. She is equated with the earth, which man then plows and plants with his seed. In this paradigm, even though woman is the giving, creative element, she is nonetheless passive. The fertilizing male plays the active role in casting his seed into her receptive womb.

The Babylonian "Hymn to Innana" drives this analogy home when it has the goddess repeatedly crying out to her lover, "Plow my vulva!" This statement at once equates the woman with the fecund field. Her vulva becomes the furrow in which the seed is planted, and the active male principle is the plow that penetrates the earth, allowing the seed to fall deep inside. As elegant and visceral as the image is, it nevertheless makes the goddess a passive figure in the role of fertilization. She is a vessel, a receptacle. Even though she is the icon of fertility itself, the masculine principle is still a force that is acting upon her, not working in tandem with her.

This way of looking at the Goddess has never really appealed to me. Archetypal woman as mother and nurturer is all well and good, but all the myths this perspective gives rise to portray her as far too passive for my liking. I can't relate to a Goddess who just lies there and lets the God plow into her over and over again. How many women who identify with an empowered Goddess archetype are going to allow that? At least from my experience, there should be activity from both ends of that exchange.

This has always left me wondering about the supposed matriarchal societies that existed throughout Eastern Europe and places like Malta, all cited in Marija Gimbutas' "Civilization of the Goddess". How could the Mother-as-Nurturer hold a position of direct authority when she was universally portrayed as the passive, receptive element of creation? Wouldn't the guidance of a culture fall more naturally to the active element associated with man if that culture were primed to look upon woman more as a receptive caregiver than anything else?

Of course, if Gimbutas's dates are to be believed (and there is controversy surrounding her entire body of work), these civilizations existed at least 9000 years ago, and possibly even more. So it should be acknowledged that it's very likely that they had a different way of looking at reality than we, in these modern times, perceive things.

One night, I was reading Olga Kharitidi's book *Entering the Circle*. This is a fascinating exposition of Kharitidi's explorations into Siberian shamanism and its asserted pre-historical roots. Towards the end of the text,

Kharitidi discusses the existence of an ancient civilization whose supposed migrations seem to match those of the Goddess Culture postulated by Gimbutas. The scholar in me had some doubts about the true historicity of everything being explained, and yet the mythic thinker in me still felt inspired. And I think sometimes its important to acknowledge that our myths do not have to be factual in order to hold truth. That being said, Kharitidi's mythic tale of the origins of Siberian shamanism held some enlightening perspectives on the idea of an active female principle.

From the issues raised by the text, I started wondering how civilizations that thought very differently from our own might look differently at the process of creation and generation. And I hit upon a paradigm of reproduction that I liked much better than the one we typically encounter in our culture. After contemplating this for a little while, it allowed me to see the notion of matriarchy in a completely different context.

Imagine, if you will, a culture where the feminine aspect is definitively the active principle in reproduction. How would this affect the myths, symbols, and very ideals of such a culture? I could see women taking active roles of authority in a culture based upon myths that present the divine feminine as a distinctly active principle. But how might the reproductive process be viewed so as to support these ideas?

Right now, our culture's myths of the "Great Mother" rely on perceiving the man as the one who plants his seed in the fecund womb. The Mother then carries the man's child within her, nurturing it with her own life force until it is ready to face the world. The roles between male and female in this view of the exchange are not balanced. The child in the womb is something woman is just carrying – that active principle of creation is still the man.

Is there another perspective that might allow the male and female principles to play more equal roles? And might one of these portray the divine feminine as the active, instead of the passive, participant?

Try looking at things not with man as Fertilizer and woman as Field, but with man as the Giver and woman as the Shaper of that gift. In this schema, the sperm given forth by the man is a raw but vital substance poured into the alchemical forge that is the active feminine. The woman then takes this raw stuff and makes something viable out of it.

In this way of looking at things, the gestation period is not a time where the mother is merely carrying around the man's child. Instead, she is actually making that child from the raw stuff provided by the man. Here the action is shared. The man acts by providing the primal clay. The woman then acts by molding this clay and shaping it into a complex, living form.

Cultures the world over depict their creator gods as potters who craft human beings upon their potter's wheels. This includes gods ranging from the Greek Prometheus to the Egyptian Khnum, as well as the Hebrew/Christian Yahweh. Adam's name means "clay" and he is given this name because his creator shapes him from the dust of the ground, moistened with spittle and quickened with breath. Invariably, these shaper gods are depicted in the masculine. Yet, looking at things from the different perspective presented above, these gods all seem to be masculinized aspects of the active feminine principle -- personifications of her very ability to shape life from her fertile substance.

This is the Goddess that I thought I *should* see: she who shapes the raw stuff of creation into a living, breathing human being. This active, shaping Goddess could easily inspire a culture to look upon its women as directors of society, and shapers of both ideals and laws. This is the Goddess whose civilization Gimbutas seems to be looking for, a powerful, active principle who does not merely carry the seed of the man but makes it uniquely her own.

Creating Living Ritual

As someone with experience running Pagan and non-denominational rituals, I have had many people approach me asking my advice on how to design, develop and run a good ritual. There are a lot of books on ritual available on the market, but the vast majority of them offer rites that the student is supposed to reproduce wholesale. As many people drawn to the neo-Pagan movement find themselves there as a reaction against indoctrinated behavior and dogma, such an approach to ritual is anathema to them. Ultimately picking up a Wiccan book of rites and following them word for word like some magickal formula is simply exchanging one dogma for another.

So what makes a good rite – a rite that avoids the potential hazard of merely trading one static system for another?

A good rite, a *living* ritual, is something which happens in the moment, something which is built by the energies and personalities of everyone who is participating in it. The person who is leading the ritual adds their own touch to it. The person for whom the ritual is being held also influences the wording, the tone, and the feel of things. And every single spectator, each person who is not directly involved in the action of the ritual but who serves as a witness and an observer, all of these people add their subtle changes, as well.

The result is a ritual which is wholly unique for that point in time and for the people who are involved in it. It is potent, and it has very profound meaning for everyone involved. It is impossible to record the words that go along with a ritual like this. The words just come. What we can record is a basic framework for what the ritual is supposed to accomplish. This serves as a guideline that the ritual priest must be familiar with – so familiar with, in fact, that he can decide, right then, on the fly, what is appropriate to focus on, what he should change, what to leave out entirely, and what may need to be inserted for the rite to have the maximum impact and meaning for everyone involved. Yet even with these on-the-fly alterations, the ritual priest must still be able to pick up where he left off, maintain the overall continuity of the ritual, and bring things to a solid and meaningful conclusion.

I call this Living Ritual. It is very similar to an improvisational performance in theater, only applied to a ritual setting. It is not an easy form of ritual to pull off, because there are so many variables involved once things get going, and there is never the easy crutch of a scripted rite to fall back upon. In order to perform a ritual like this, the ritual priest must have an excellent sense of timing and a keen ability to judge people.

He should know a good deal about people's emotional reactions, and how to maximize upon those in ritual space. He should know what symbols and phrases are meaningful not only to the individual but to the group as a whole, and he must know how to manipulate these for maximum effect. A background in theater certainly helps.

Ritual means nothing if it does not impact us upon a very profound level. But everyone who has chosen to participate in that ritual has asked to be affected on that level, and through their shared participation, they also serve to heighten that level, pushing it to an even more intense state. The group comes together as a whole, opening themselves up to deeper experiences, to spiritual revelation and emotion, and it is the responsibility of the ritual priest to understand this, understand what is needed, and to guide the rite toward that end.

All of this makes the ritual sound like some kind of psychodrama. But there's nothing wrong with being a little theatrical with your rituals. The Western theatrical tradition comes down to us not from stages that were meant to merely amuse, but from the Greek tradition of dramatic ritual that was part of the yearly Eleusinian mysteries. Theater and ritual have always gone hand in hand. Recreational theater still has a phenomenal impact on the emotional and mental state of those who observe it, not to mention those who actually are involved in the performance. It is a potent psychological tool, and why would something this profound be used merely for recreation when it can be harnessed and used to affect a more personal spiritual response in observers and participants?

Ritual is about stepping out of our ordinary space and crossing the threshold to something more profound. Think about going to the movies. When you enter the theater, you have made an agreement with the people behind the picture: you are going to suspend your disbelief, and for the course of the movie, the trials and triumphs, the joys and fears of the characters on the screen are going to become, at least for a little while, more real to you than your own life. You are going to live, for two hours, vicariously through them, and you will come away as if you had actually experienced all of those emotions yourself. Participating in a shared reality like that speaks to us on a very deep level. And in ritual, we are not just simply stepping through the doors and entering that Other space for the sake of recreation. We are stepping into a shared space with others who are important to us, to celebrate ideas that are important to us, and to strive toward something which we believe is nothing less than sacred. There is nothing more potent or more personally transformative than an experience of that kind.

So you see, a ritual priest has a very great responsibility to fulfill. He has to not only maintain that feeling of Other space, that sense of the sacred, in a general way, but he must also maintain the heightened sense of reality that everyone has come to the ritual to experience for each individual person. This requires a massive amount of presence and charisma on his part, as well as a very deep understanding of how the energies in such a group work, how to harness them, focus them, and keep them cycling through everyone so there is no lull in the intensity. Living Ritual is a direct, intense, and immediate experience. It is not only a very personal sort of ritual, but it is also a very *personalized* ritual. Which is why it must change moment to moment, as the need for such change arises, and why no one ritual, even if the framework and overall intent is the same, can be repeated precisely the way it was in a time before.

Tips for Creating Living Ritual

So how do you go about writing a Living Ritual? Well, we've found that you first have to throw out your expectations of what a ritual should look like, at least on the written page. There's just no neat way to write down one of these rituals, and even if you try, you're going to wind up rewriting it almost completely the very next time you hold that particular rite. If you do write one down, you're going to end up with something that looks more like a collection of rough notes, possibly with diagrams and a few isolated bits of dialogue that you will hope retain some semblance of their wording when applied to the actual rite.

Sound chaotic? Of course it does, but this is what it should be. You need to have just enough order in place to account for the natural chaos that will inevitably occur. A static script cannot possibly bend in the directions you will need it to bend if you are going to achieve true Living Ritual. What you need is a framework which you can build upon once you are actually involved in the ritual itself. This framework should be designed to be flexible but it should also have stable enough parameters that you have a clear beginning, middle, and end to the ritual. Everything in between really will depend upon what you want to accomplish with the ritual, what it's meant to celebrate, how many people are going to be involved, and what symbols and language you will need for the maximum impact of the rite.

As a general rule, the beginning of a ritual is marked by two things: establishing community and establishing the purpose of the ritual. These two things can be part and parcel of the same speech which opens the ritual, although this is not always the case. The middle of the ritual is a peak in the ritual action. It is a focal point of interest, where the main purpose of the rite achieves a climax and can then begin moving toward resolution. This is usually accompanied by some overt ritual action which acknowledges that climax and which marks it as special for everyone involved. The end of the ritual is when things conclude. The climactic point of the rite is given resolution. The ritual priest offers an interpretation or explanation for why what has just been shared is important to the community. He takes the climax out of the realm of the individual and makes it something that is pertinent on a communal level. This is the point where even the observers to the ritual are given meaning which they can attach personally to what has just occurred.

Establishing community is usually achieved through a group prayer or charge which covers the basic beliefs that are shared by the community. These basic beliefs are the identity of the community. They are the mortar which hold the individual members together, and they are why each of those individual persons has chosen to participate in this rite in the first place, and share something special with everyone else.

Establishing purpose usually takes the form of a proclamation. The ritual priest explains why everyone has gathered together and what specifically is to be separated. If the ritual is something which focuses on one individual, such as a rite of passage, then that individual is brought forward and acknowledged as the focal point of the action to come.

A great deal can vary from here on out depending on the purpose of the ritual, the symbol system of the people involved, and the technique of the ritual priest. In general, there is action, and it moves toward a climax. This action involves spoken words, and the main dialogue will be that of the leading priest, but others will very likely have spoken parts as well, as they respond to the dialogue of the priest. Ritual actions may occur here, such as the taking of vows or the sharing of wine. Very rarely is this simply dialogue – an actual physical action which represents the ideas and beliefs expressed in the dialogue at this time has a very potent affect. It is a ritualized action, and as such it becomes a symbol for the meaning of the entire ritual. Usually the climax occurs when this ritual action takes place.

From the point of the ritual action, there is more dialogue which interprets and explains what just occurred. Blessings may occur here, or words of advice, or songs, or something else which takes the specific action(s) and puts it in the realm of individual meaning for every person present. The opening was an affirmation of why that group has something to share. You should not achieve closure with the ritual until everyone has actually shared something to reinforce that feeling of community.

Of course, this framework gives you a lot of room for improvisation. Sometimes it's hard to fill in those spaces, especially because there are no real guidelines for what is appropriate and what is not. On the whole, it is much easier for the ritual priest to just recite something out of a book, but it will never have the direct and personal impact that a living ritual can have. With a book or a memorized script, you are not in danger of saying the wrong thing. When put on the spot, however, things get said that maybe you never intended, but they are almost always the truth. They are spoken from the heart, in the heat of the moment, with all the masks we ordinarily wear stripped away. This, above all else, is the real source of power in Living Ritual. It forces us to be ourselves in the middle of the ritual space. There are no pretty words we can rely on except what we pull up out of our own hearts. No book or set formula exists to serve as a barrier between the leading priest and everyone else. It is all raw, immediate, and just the way it is.

Below you will find some questions that may help you when designing a living ritual of your own. They don't necessarily cover everything, but they should make you think enough about the ritual you are planning to probably come up with the questions that were missed.

What is the purpose of the ritual?

People come together to celebrate ritual for all manner of things. Usually, the main purpose of ritual is to mark a rite of passage. Marriages, baptisms, funerals, all of these are rites of passage. They mark a transition from one state to the next. A rite of dedication or the passing from level of initiation to the next, these are rites of passage as well.

Another purpose for ritual is to commemorate an event. Perhaps your group gets together every year to celebrate their founding. That would be a commemoration. Seasonal rituals commemorate events, although these usually aren't events as we think of them in a mundane sense, such as an anniversary, so much as a celebration which is tied to myth. Christmas commemorates the birth of Christ. Independence Day commemorates the "birth" of the United States.

If a ritual is not intended to mark a rite of passage or to commemorate an event, then it is probably just a community ritual. Community rituals are no less important that the other two types discussed above. In some respects, they are far more important, because they are what help to build the sense of unity and shared purpose within the group that holds it together. A very loose version of a community ritual is an annual family reunion. Everyone gets together and celebrates their bond as a family. Traditional meals are shared, traditional games are played. No one calls it a ritual, but that doesn't make it any less potent or significant. Community is why the other types of ritual hold any kind of significance for us in the first place.

What kind if meaning is it supposed to have?

What do you want people to go away with from this ritual? Keeping in mind that the emotional level of sacred space is significantly heightened, determined what kinds of emotions you want to evoke in people. Is this ritual one of pure celebration, or is it meant to be a ritual of atonement, where everyone seriously reevaluates their lives and determines what needs to be let go. Is this a ritual of farewell? Is it something that will involve more than one strong kind of emotion, like a funeral where the life of the deceased is celebrated at the same time that his loved ones say farewell?

The emotional content of the ritual is very important, because you have to be prepared for intense reactions. It is not uncommon for people in ritual – even celebratory ritual – to be moved to tears. It is your responsibility to make certain that the language and tone of the rite is respectful of that, and that, by the end of the ritual, there is some kind of emotional closure for everyone, so they can go away feeling better about things. Catharsis is a power and transformative tool, but only because the person going through it feels cleansed at the end.

Who will be involved in running the ritual?

Who do you have to play the main parts in the ritual? Who will be the leading priest, and what are his strengths or weaknesses? Does he have the presence and charisma to pull the ritual off? If it is a very potently emotional ritual, this is a crucial consideration. Some community rituals are pretty light-hearted affairs, and it won't have a negative impact on anyone if the leading priest is also light-hearted about the rite. But a priest who cannot maintain the solemnity and respect required for a more somber ritual, such as a funeral, may actually hurt the ritual. The rite is only as powerful as the people involved in it, and it certainly only has what power those people allow it to have, but the keystone for this power, the central pillar that must be able to hold it all up is the priest. If the priest is weak, then no matter what effort the other participants may make, the overall ritual can crumble.

Who will this ritual be open to?

Carefully consider who you will and will not allow to the ritual. Some rituals cannot be open to the public. Some rituals are so intensely personal, only the priest, the person involved, and a few hand-selected friends can participate if things are going to go smoothly. There is a level of trust that each participant must achieve in order to truly let go and experience all that the ritual has to offer. If the presence of just one person shatters that trust, then the ritual looses that much potency.

Respect is also a very important thing to consider among those who may potentially participate in a ritual. Some rituals, like celebrations of community, can be open to children or individuals at any level of initiation into the group. But other rituals deal with much more profound ideas and beliefs. These ideas and beliefs hold great significance for the people celebrating them, or else they wouldn't be celebrating them in a ritual at all. Do not disrespect the sanctity of those beliefs by allowing people who either do not understand those beliefs or who cannot show them the respect they deserve in the confines of the ritual. This sets a precedent for some exclusivity in ritual, but the fact of the matter is, especially where beliefs are concerned, some things are exclusive. You do not want to expose a raw initiate to the mystery of mysteries – not because that is a great secret of the faith, but because a raw initiate probably won't even know what it is he's looking at.

What symbols do you want to use?

Symbols, phrases, and style of language can be very crucial to a ritual. Symbols, of course, have to be pertinent to the group in order to have any meaning. If a group is organized enough in its beliefs and its sense of community to be holding rituals, chances are it already has a number of established symbols which have significance for its beliefs and its community. Symbols like this add power to the ritual by giving everyone present a convenient focus for the ideas and beliefs which the symbol represents. If an Otherkin ritual is being held, no one needs to explain the meaning of the Septagram. The entire group understands the meanings, and part of that understanding defines them as a group in the first place. The Septagram then, like the Christian Cross, serves as a representation of the common beliefs of those gathered in the ritual.

As a group develops its own feel, certain phrases, words, or types of language also become part of that group's identity. When designing a ritual for that group, it is your responsibility to be familiar with these words and what they mean, not just on the surface but on a symbolic level as well. If there are specific prayers or standard responses, such as "So Mote It Be," which hold great significance for everyone present, then these should be worked into the rite. A lot of this really deals with the unique identity of the group for whom the ritual is tailored, but the basic idea is you're not going to conclude a Wiccan prayer with "Amen" and expect all the participants to resonate with that. The importance of the words is what the community attaches to them, and if the community attaches no importance, then there will be less of an impact when those words are used in ritual.

What tools do you want to use?

This again is a concern which is very dependent upon the beliefs and symbol system in place within the context of the community. What tools are ordinarily used by the members of the community, especially when delineating their sacred lives from the mundane. For example, do individuals within the community tend to light candles when they are meditating? Then candles should probably be lit for the duration of the ritual. Do members of the community tend to use incense to clear and declare their sacred space? Then incense should also be used as part of the ritual.

Some communities have very involved tools, and these have as much meaning and impact as the basic faith-symbols of the group. Wine, shared as a ritual drink, is a very symbolic ritual tool, and it finds its way into rites from Judaism to Christianity, and even to Wicca. Some tools can even be symbols in and of themselves, such as the wand in Wicca or the compass in Freemasonry. These are actual objects which can be used physically or symbolically during the course of the ritual which have deep meaning for the participants.

If you use a ritual tool, you of course need to understand what it means. The tool has significance because it represents something, and that representation must be pertinent within the context of the ritual. You're not going to have someone jump over the broom in a baptismal rite. That has meaning only for weddings, unless for some reason your particular group has totally reworked the meaning of that tool.

Some groups prefer to work without any ritual tools, but as covered above, even candles and incense fall under this category, and these can be found in practically every religion the world over. So consider carefully the content of the ritual and the impact certain actions need to have. If having a physical object can help reinforce the meaning of that content and those actions, then by all means use it in the rite. Just try not to get bogged down in tools. When not used properly, ritual tools can be very distracting. Too many ritual tools tend to obscure the ritual rather than clarify and accent its meaning.

How do you want people to feel after the ritual?

This goes along with the emotional content you want to cover in the ritual, but it also impacts how you want to achieve closure with that impact. As discussed above, when done correctly, Living Ritual evokes a very powerful emotional response from the participants. You need to figure out where you want this response to take people, how you want them to leave the ritual and take it out into their lives. You really need to understand the psychology of your group in order to answer this question. You need to know what kind of emotional release they might need, and to what level that might be healthy. You need to be able to judge how far things should go, and you need to be able to pull it all back together into a meaningful whole. A lot of thought should go into this, and into the whole experience of the ritual, because of the deep psychological, spiritual, and emotional affects you can have on your participants with your rites.

This is nothing to take lightly, and you should always consider what you are trying to accomplish with as much wisdom and maturity as you can muster. Ritual is supposed to improve people's lives. It is intended to show them new aspects of themselves, help them to let go of old ways of being, and in general give them a tangible transformative experience that they can hold onto when they return to their everyday lives. That might seem like a tall order to fill, but I've seen it done. I've done it myself. And in the end, there is nothing more rewarding than feeling the impact that you have had on everyone in guiding them through this deeply meaningful experience. It's an accomplishment, and it's worth all the care and effort and stage fright you might have to endure when planning something real.

The Doctrine of Free Will

I am a strong advocate of the doctrine of free will. Free will, to me, means that each individual has a right to choose the direction of his or her life. This means that individuals have the right to choose the expression of their religious beliefs, the expression of the sexual orientation, the expression of their personal fashion - in short, they have the right to choose what they do with themselves and their life. I view free will as an inarguable human right, and as chaotic as the truest application of that doctrine can make the world, I still think it is the fundamental rule we should all abide by.

In respecting free will, I acknowledge that I have a right to make decisions about my own life. Whether they are the right or wrong decisions, they are still mine to make. And I acknowledge that I do not have the right to dictate what is right or wrong for anyone else. They are not me and I am not them, therefore, it is impossible to apply what is right and wrong for one to the other. That would be like an orange faulting an apple for having a smooth, red skin and an apple faulting an orange for having a thick, bumpy rind. The value system from one to the other just does not apply.

Now, I also acknowledge that it would be naïve to think that one's personal choices do not affect others. Everything each person does has a ripple effect upon the world around them. In the case of individuals closest to the person in question, personal choices can have a very intense impact. A young man's choice to come out of the closet will obviously have a much greater impact on his current girlfriend than it will have on some business man in Japan. However, the reaction one may take to this impact is also a matter of personal choice. The girlfriend, to continue the example, may decide to take this revelation very personally, presume it means that she somehow had an influence on her boyfriend's inherent "gayness" and choose never to date a man again for fear of also turning him gay.

Clearly, in this example, she is choosing to over-react to her boyfriend's coming out, and that choice is based upon a number of assumptions she has also chosen to draw from the whole ordeal. Some other girlfriend might simply choose to accept the revelation for what it is, be happy for her boyfriend, and help him pick out a likely partner.

The bottom line here is, all of our choices affect everyone around us. And the way in which each of us chooses to react to these choices also affects everyone around us. This is part of the reciprocal nature of reality. Every action has a reaction. The only way to avoid having an impact - negative or otherwise - on the world around you would be to never act at all. And from a Jain perspective, not acting would have to include not even breathing, since in breathing there is always a chance that you might inhale and kill some hapless organism.

To never act and to never choose simply out of the fear of being wrong or of causing some kind of harm is to be paralyzed utterly into inaction. It is to not live. Yet even the choice to never act is still a choice in and of itself.

What all of this comes down to, is we all have the right to make our own choices. None of us have the right to make choices for others. In making our choices, it is best to consider the impact these choices may have upon others, but the very fact that there is an impact should not be a reason not to make a choice. It is certainly not a reason to take the option for a choice away. Also, in assuming that others will respect our own choices, we also must extend our own respect, regardless of our personal agreement with the choice.

I know myself, and I know my life, and even then I don't always make the best decisions about my choices. How then can I even presume to make choices for others when I cannot know who they are at the core or what it's like to live their lives? I cannot even judge whether or not the choices I see them making are right or wrong for them, as the same criterion for right and wrong do not apply to both them and me. I cannot know. I cannot judge.

In respecting free will and personal choice, I admit this and respect it. But I also hope that others will respect it as well. I seek to make my own choices unhindered by the judgment of others. They are not me. They cannot know what is right or wrong for me. They should not judge.

At its most basic, this is all just the Golden Rule. It is the best and the wisest rule: "Do unto others as you would have them do unto you." If you value freedom, allow others their choice. If you don't agree with everyone else's judgments and rules, don't seek to impose yours upon others. All of us, of course, affect one another with our choices. This cannot be avoided. It's called life. Let's all participate fairly and try to learn something from one another.

Mystic and Madman: the Shaman as a Traveler Between Realities

In the simplest sense of the word, a shaman is the member of his community who stands at the threshold of two distinct states of existence. On one hand, he is a member of the earthly community, existing with all other men in ordinary reality. He hunts and fishes, weaves baskets, and attends to the same worldly concerns as any other member of the community. And yet he also exists in nonordinary reality; he speaks with spirits, journeys to the realm of the dead and returns unharmed, obtains gifts and favors from gods, and interacts with a realm of existence which lies far beyond the boundaries of ordinary reality. He serves as an intermediary between his community and an aspect of their world that they cannot willingly contact. Ultimately, he performs this role because no one else in the community is equipped either emotionally or spiritually to do so.

The shaman has access to this numinous level of reality through his ability to enter a unique trance-state, often termed the shamanic state of consciousness, or SSC. This trance-state allows the shaman to leave his body and travel through the many non-physical and supra-physical levels of reality. While in this state, the shaman can communicate with totem animals, gods, demons, and the spirits of the dead. The shamanic trance-state has been compared by some writers, such as Richard Noll, to the hallucinatory states associated with mental illness, such as schizophrenia. And yet, unlike a traditional schizophrenic, the shaman can willfully enter and depart from this altered state of consciousness. It is the volitionary aspect of the SSC, more than anything else, that sets it apart from states of consciousness traditionally associated with mental illness.

There are myths in many of the cultures in which shamanism is practiced which tell of a far away time when all men were shamans (Eliade, 483). During this ideal time of the distant past, the bridge between the world of men and the world of spirits was open to all who wished to cross. Then mankind, for one reason or another, fell away from that universal state of spiritual connectedness, and only the shaman retained contact with the bridge between the realities.

This bridge is a crucial point in shamanic cosmology. In some cultures it is represented as a central tent pole that runs through the earthly realm, connecting it to the celestial realm above and the underworld below. In other cultures it is represented as the World Tree. In still others, the *axis mundi* takes the form of sacred a central mountain (often with the World Tree growing from its summit) (Eliade, 259 -- 269).

Regardless of the symbol assigned to it, the concept remains the same; it is the center of the created cosmos, the common point that allows access to all the other levels of reality. The shaman's ability to enter the unique state of consciousness hinges upon his ability to reach this central point and travel along it to the many worlds it runs through.

It is a common assumption that all shamans practice the ritual ingestion of hallucinogens. The most familiar hallucinogenic agents taken by shamans are the peyote cactus and the psilocybin mushroom though quite a number of self-proclaimed modern shamans make use of the synthetic hallucinogen LSD. While it cannot be denied that hallucinogens play a role in shamanic practices, it should be noted that such hallucinogens are never taken casually by the shaman. The Huichol Indians undertake a long and arduous journey in search of the peyote cactus, and the peyote buttons are ingested only as the culmination of a very lengthy and involved communal ritual. This is typical of the serious attitude shamans have toward their hallucinogenic agents.

In most cases, a lengthy period of fasting and meditation has preceded the ingestion of the hallucinogenic agent. Often, at least one other shaman experienced in the matters of hallucinogens remains by the side of the shaman who has ingested the agent to deal with any unforeseen problems which may arise. Further, the shaman taking the hallucinogen is aware that his action represents a certain amount of risk; while under the influence of the hallucinogen, the individual is especially vulnerable to spiritual attack. His body may become possessed by evil spirits and those self-same spirits may rip his very soul out by the roots and carry it off until it becomes lost within the realm of the dead. Only another experienced shaman would be able to retrieve the lost soul, and even then, he would be putting himself at considerable risk.

Hallucinogens are but one of the many methods used by shamans to achieve the SSC. The shaman is certainly not limited in his tools for achieving his unique trance state to merely hallucinogenic agents. He may use any one of a number of techniques to cross the bridge and embark upon the shamanic journey. Each technique is intended to increase the vividness of the shaman's inner vision, ultimately propelling him into the SSC. Most methods are monotonous and to a large extent physically taxing. The shaman may engage in long periods of dancing, ascetic practices which induce pain stimulation, dehydration, hypoglycemia, or sleep deprivation (Noll, 1987: 49).

Such dramatic methods of achieving the trance-state are as potentially dangerous to body, mind, and spirit as ingesting hallucinogens, but like hallucinogens, they facilitate the move from ordinary reality to non-ordinary reality. The journey from ordinary consciousness to the SSC does not always have to be as dangerous or as physically demanding, however. The simplest and most common tool used by the shaman to enter the shamanic state of consciousness is the monotonous rhythm of the drum. Indeed there is a growing number of modern shamans who look down upon those of their number who adopt more theatrical and severe methods, suggesting that such techniques are most often used "by the people who are unable to make the journey with the drum alone" (Harner, 1988: 12).

The simple, monotonous rhythm of the drum is by far "the most common vehicle of the shaman's journey" (Harner, 1988: 12). While any of the above techniques may be used to achieve a visionary trance-state, the tool for entering the SSC that is particular to the shaman is the drum. Known as the "shaman's horse" or the "shaman's roebuck," the drum is not only the figurative steed which carries him into the SSC, it represents the central point to which and through which he must travel (Eliade, 173 -- 174).

Traditionally, the shaman's drum is made from a single round of wood with animal skin stretched over one side. The drum itself is approached as if it were a living entity: it has a spirit of its own, and this spirit is connected mystically to the shaman who uses that particular drum. In some cultures, this connection is seen as being so profound that not only can no other shaman use the drum, but when that particular shaman passes away, his drum is symbolically "killed" as well.

The drum may by painted inside and out with symbols which represent aspects of the shaman's power. It may be decorated with a map of the cosmos, with each point along the shaman's journey pictorially represented, and it may be further adorned with stones, shells, beads, feathers, and other such objects which, endowed with a power of their own, add to the whole of the shaman's power. But while the decorations of the drum and their significance vary from culture to culture, it is universally acknowledged that the drum is the seat of the shaman's power to travel between the worlds (Eliade, 169 -- 173).

The drum is typically constructed of the wood of the World Tree. The species of this tree varies culturally, but universally it is seen as a kind of living, central pillar that stands between the many levels of reality, providing access to all of them. In the myths of many shamanic cultures, this tree is further the seat of the Cosmic Lord, a being often depicted as the theriomorphic ancestor of all mankind (Eliade, 169). Through its symbolic connection to the Cosmic Tree, the drum comes to represent the tree itself. The animal skin of the drum serves to connect the shaman to the theriomorphic deity of the tree. Thus, when the shaman uses the drum, it connects him through a process of sympathetic magic to the World Tree, bringing him into a state of union with the theriomorphic ancestor. Through this union he can then exercise the powers of the deity: he gains awareness of all the levels of reality and, most importantly, the ability to move between them (Eliade, 171).

The drum, as part of the Cosmic Tree serves as a portal to that tree which connects the shaman to the center of the world. Once there, the shaman himself becomes lord of the tree. Standing at the point where all things converge, he has the ability to be anywhere and to see anything he pleases. Through his ability to enter a unique and controlled altered state, the shaman transcends the limits of space and time and enters into mystical union with the whole of the created cosmos.

Integrating the Jungian Shadow

In the early 20th century, a man by the name of Carl Jung conceived of something he called the "shadow". Carl Jung was a psychologist, in fact, he was a student of Freud, and he was searching for a term to describe those dark spaces in everyone's psyche that all of us have but none of us like to admit are there.

The shadow, Jung believed, was a source of great drive and inspiration for people. Yet it was also a place where we kept many repressed impulses and fears. When it was dealt with correctly, a healthy psyche could make use of the energy and insights stored there. When it was denied and buried, it came out in really nasty behaviors and psychoses. Jung was a proponent of understanding the shadow, no matter how dark and scary it looked to our everyday minds. He felt we really couldn't be whole without it. But since our mainstream culture attaches such significance to darkness and makes it something we should fear and fight and feel guilty about, not a whole lot is done with the shadow these days.

In the Kheprian tradition, there is an underlying current of darkness that some people may find a little scary and intimidating. But the darkness that emerges in our teachings is not an evil darkness or even a destructive one. It is simply an aspect of the integrated shadow. Like Jung, we believe that if you get acquainted with your shadow and make it a part of your Self, then you have nothing to fear from it. You can work with its impulses, and you can choose whether or not to act upon the drives it conveys to you. It is only when the shadow is unknown and suppressed that it can control our behaviors in a destructive manner, but unfortunately suppressing the shadow and denying its existence is the norm for most of Western culture.

What is the use of getting to know your darkness? Isn't exploring those unsavory aspects of your Self fixating on them and encouraging them to come out in your daily life? Think of it like this: you live in a house with an unfinished basement. Whenever you have something in your house that you don't really use anymore but you don't quite want to throw away, you box it up and put it down in the basement. Over the course of many years, all manner of things get stored down there. After a while, there are so many boxes, you're not even sure what you have in your basement anymore. A lot of it's junk, the detritus of your daily life. Yet there are also some useful and very valuable things down there too, mixed up with and hidden among the junk.

Of course, all the boxes that have piled up over the years have attracted bugs and spiders and other crawly things.

There are cobwebs and who knows what living in the cardboard and old newspapers down there. Some things have gotten moldy, some things outright stink. But, especially if you ever want to find the good things that are stored there among the garbage, you are going to eventually have to clean your basement out. You will have to pull out all the boxes and sift by hand through the junk, dust, spiders, cobwebs and all.

Throughout this enterprise, if you are afraid to get dirty, you are not going to last very long. If you let the appearance of a little spider send you running, you might miss the valuable antique that was waiting to be uncovered in the next box over. And if, like most people, you let the fact that your basement is dark and dank and a little spooky get to you, you'll probably never clean the boxes out at all.

In Jungian terms, the house represents your Self. The basement is your shadow. It's the dark place in your psyche where you put things you don't want to look at anymore. Aspects of your personality that disturb you, but which you just can't seem to throw away (kind of like that gaudy lamp your Aunt Edna bought you that one Christmas years ago) all get boxed up and shoved down in the dark recesses of your shadow. And some things that get shoved there in the darkness get ugly. They molder and sprout things that don't look natural anymore; they attract darker little things, creepy-crawlies that might just come sneaking up the stairs into the respectable portion of your home when you're not paying attention. That's the price of repression, you see: put it away somewhere that you can't see it, and the moment you forget that it's there, it will choose the time and the place that is comes creeping out of the darkness into your ordinary life.

Not everything in your shadow is nasty and ugly. But very little of it is shiny and bright. In order to have a whole personality, you have to be brave enough to go down into your personal basement and sort through all the boxes -- dust, spiders, cobwebs and all. If you are going to ever throw out any of the really nasty things, then you have to pull them out and face them and ultimately understand why you can't use them anymore. And if you are going to find those hidden treasures that are part and parcel of your gloomy psychological basement, you have to spend enough time looking at them and dusting them off in order to realize their intrinsic worth.

You cannot be afraid. The fear and the darkness are really things that we have put there on our own. We make our own basements, and it's important to realize that just as the basement is still an integral part of your house, so too is your shadow an integral part of your Self. Some really paranoid folk might lock the basement door and cover it with boards, or even brick it up, but what happens when you've got to get to the water heater or the furnace? You've just shut yourself out of something essential to the healthy functioning of your home.

The darkness that your shadow embodies is not an evil darkness. It is simply another aspect of the light. One cannot be whole without the other. And we cannot be whole without both.

Accepting the Extraordinary in Our Everyday Lives

If you've done any kind of studying about magick or the occult on the Internet, you've seen it. Some site which proclaims to have the "one truth" about magick, usually as revealed through scrolls or tablets of immeasurable age. These scrolls or tablets or hidden teachings were originally written in some obscure tongue (maybe Egyptian, maybe Sumerian, maybe Enochian or something "never encountered before"). Further, they were either recently unearthed in some unpronounceable country, or they had been discovered quite some time ago and suppressed, or they have simply been passed down for generations through a super-secret organization of ascended immortals who suddenly felt the need to reveal themselves through a tacky-looking web-page. Without looking very hard, you can find such sites all over the Wiccan and Pagan communities, the Otherkin communities, Vampire and Gothic subcultures, not to mention New Age, Metaphysical, Christian, or insert-the-religion-of-the-week here. Everyone claims to have the "one truth", and everyone claims it is secret, and mysterious, and hundreds (if not thousands) of years old.

I usually read through sites like this just out of curiosity. And sometimes I am pleasantly surprised by the validity of the information I find there (although admittedly this is a pretty rare occurrence). And I always end up asking myself, why start off with a lie just to validate your beliefs? Take out the bogus claims of a connection to an ancient and never before heard of secret society, remove the affectation that the thoroughly modern writings are merely translations of some ancient and obscure artifact, delete the pretension that the speaker is actually a 3000-year-old "truly immortal" demon-incarnated-in-human-flesh or whatever, and sometimes there's some good stuff there. Somebody thought it up and had the motivation to write it down. But they just didn't have the self-confidence to claim it as their own.

Why go through the trouble of fabricating a barely believable origin story just to communicate your spiritual beliefs? I'll admit, peoples' belief factor in something is usually pretty low unless they are told that it can be traced to a tradition practiced however many millennia ago. It's a precedent set by the Bible and other sacred scriptures. I've seen a certain amount of smug satisfaction among the Christians when they're engaged in a religious debate with a newer faith and they're able to just point to the Bible and say, "See, what I believe *must* be true because somebody wrote it down two thousand years ago." But that's a weak argument. Truthfully, it's a cop-out. Why not believe in something just because you believe it? Isn't that the nature of belief anyway?

But people seem to need their crutch of validation. Usually, the claim that something is ancient is enough to inspire faith in most people. In religions and spirituality, somehow age makes even the most ridiculous claims feasible. If some guy were to travel across America today, preaching peace and brotherly love and asking guys to abandon their families, leave their jobs, become essentially homeless, and follow him, he'd be put away pretty quickly. That is, if anyone even bothered to follow him at all. But Jesus was a radical in his day. Two thousand years of idealization tends to make most of us forget that. The Buddha sat under to Bodhi tree for years, starving himself nearly to death. He ate a single hemp seed each day to sustain himself. Our modern response? We'd probably call a psychiatrist and have him dragged away and force fed. He's be prosecuted later for growing the pot that yielded his nourishing seeds.

And yet these are fathers of ancient and well-respected religious traditions. We tend not to question their teachings based on age and familiarity alone. And in this, they set a precedent of belief. Buddhism and Christianity are accepted as valid by many just on the basis of age alone. The Christ and the Buddha weren't lunatics simply because they were off doing their quirky things hundreds if not thousands of years ago. It's allowable for weird things like that to happen in the age of miracles, just as long as that age of miracles is a nice, comfortable distance from our lives today. As far as our culture is concerned, enlightened masters have to have been dead for a couple millennia before we even take them seriously. So of course newer religions can't compete. There's none of that comfortable distance of time between the followers and the origin of the beliefs.

That's how you end up with people like Joseph Smith, the founder of Mormonism. Joe had some ideas about how to reform Christianity to fit his time and culture. Some of the ideas aren't too bad, but they differed from accepted tradition. Rather than just speaking his mind and trying to convince people that his new interpretation was valid, Joe had to make up a story to make things seem divinely inspired. And so we have the angel Moroni (yes, *Moroni*) who came down to Joe one day with some golden tablets. On these tablets was the Book of Mormon. Joe wasn't allowed to keep the tablets (I seriously doubt he would have been able to carry them without hurting himself anyway) and so Moroni had him copy the divine text down before he took them back up to Heaven. Thus, the Book of Mormon became an injunction from God and not just some good ideas thought up by John. Would people have believed in it as much if it had been "The Book of Mormon, by Joseph Smith" as opposed to "Joe Smith's humble copy of the Mystic Golden Tablets of the Angel Moroni"? We'll never know.

The Wiccans and Pagans aren't any braver than Joe. They're still arguing about the Old Religion and how far back the Goddess Tradition really goes. Gerald Gardener came up with some really good ideas, but he couldn't take credit for them himself. He had to say that they had been revealed to him by a nice old witch from his village and that she had gotten the teachings herself from a long line of witches that had been practicing their very Gardnerian brand of witchcraft for hundreds of years in the English countryside.

But I won't just pick on Gerald. He's hardly alone in his insecurity. The fellows who founded the Hermetic Order of the Golden Dawn back in 1888 couldn't take credit for the exercises or metaphysical theories they developed themselves either. Here again, a mysterious lady came into the picture along with encrypted documents of an indeterminate age. This time the lady was from Germany and no one really knew how old her tradition was. But somehow, attributing the material to her, and not to Mathers and the rest who actually founded the Golden Dawn, made it seem more valid. Even Helena

Petrovna Blavatsky, a mysterious woman in her own right who generally had no fear of speaking her mind, was not brave enough to claim her metaphysical ideas as strictly her own. In her case it wasn't an angel who appeared to her and revealed the truth; it was the "secret masters", mysterious men from a mysterious part of the world who didn't even have a proper physical existence. At least in Blavatsky's case people couldn't go through the local records and learn whether or not the "masters" she named actually existed. Gardner's teacher seems to have been a complete figment, and the Golden Dawn's Anna Sprengel is still hotly debated.

And it's not just the newcomers to the religious scene. Even the Christians have fallen prey to this need for validation. They might have their Bible to thump when they feel spiritually insecure, but not all of them are completely comforted by the Good Book. There are a lot of inconsistencies in the Bible, and through modern eyes, many of the Bible's miracles seem a little hard to swallow. And so you have the scientific validators: the people who subject the Shroud of Turin to endless scientific tests in an attempt to prove that it really was the burial shroud of Jesus Christ. The archaeologists who are still looking for the actual site of Noah's Ark on the top of some great mountain in the Middle East. The folks who dug up ancient Jericho, trying to prove that the famous wall did indeed come tumbling down, just like in the story. There was a huge movement in the 19th century among archaeologists to scientifically prove the validity of Biblical claims, and to a certain extent the movement still exists today. So many religious people are not comfortable with their faith unless they can point at something solid and concrete and say, "There! This is why I believe!"

But why do we have to have proof? Trying to find solid scientific evidence for a spiritual belief strikes me as about as silly as trying to make up some incredible reason for why it must be believed. It's not a matter of proof or validity. It's a matter of faith.

Making up a fake angel to explain why you suddenly wrote a very different interpretation of Christianity is not only silly – it's insulting to yourself. I respect a lot of Wiccan ideas, but I'd respect Gerald Gardner a lot more if he'd just come out and said that he dreamed things up on his own. Would it make things less true to know that some modern person had a flash of insight? If that insight resonates with truth, why question where or how it came? Spirituality speaks to each and everyone of us in our own tongue. And it's not like spirituality stopped speaking to people a thousand or two thousand years ago (although it could be argued that many of us have forgotten how to listen). It's a constant dialogue. Everything has *not* been said. Everything *cannot* be said. Spirituality changes as we change if it's to have any validity at all, and it's a crying shame that our culture has primed us to only accept beliefs that are thousands of years out of date.

Belief is trusting in something that cannot be proven. Faith is what takes over when accepted methods of knowing fail and yet you still know that it is true. From the commentary you've read above, it's no secret that I'm a skeptic. But I'm a skeptic with faith. I believe in the heart of something if it rings true for me. The pretty decorations most people need to put on their beliefs in order to make them presentable don't interest me, and they don't fool me either. They're just costuming and they're hardly what is important. If a belief rings true, it doesn't matter if it was found scribed upon an ancient tablet from the Cradle of Civilization or if it was dreamed up by a sixteen-year-old just yesterday. It's still true.

That's not to say that you should approach every new doctrine and "take it on faith" in the old Christian way – where you were expected to swallow everything you were fed and the very act of questioning it was considered a sin. Always question whether what you're being told is true! There are many paths to knowledge where soul and Divinity are concerned. What might be true for one person might not be true for you. I don't imagine you've put any holes in your skull to let the evil spirits of headache out recently, but there was a time when this treatment was believed to work and trepanation was relatively common. Truth is not a static thing, and it changes over time, not just culturally, but for the individual, too, as he or she changes and grows.

Religious and spiritual truths are things that you have to determine for yourself. Only you know the path to Divinity that you must follow; only you can judge what appeals to your sense of faith. Consider the words of others, but reserve the final judgment of faith and belief for yourself.

The Quagmire of Spiritual Relativism

The Buddhist ideal is the Middle Path. Although I am not a Buddhist myself, I respect and support this approach to reality. I have found that it can be applied to just about every aspect of our lives.

When we exist at extremes, we cause trouble for ourselves. This holds true for attitudes and ideals as well as behaviors. Tolerance is a good example. For the most part, we exist in a society that does not practice tolerance nearly enough. The extreme of intolerance is the rule of the day. People are judged upon superficialities like appearance, hairstyle, and what music they listen to, not to mention skin color, gender, orientation, and beliefs.

Many of us, as we come from marginalized minorities, have made a concerted effort to move away from intolerance and instead to accept a person for who and what they are – whatever that may be. This is especially true when it comes to tolerance of religious and spiritual diversity.

However, all too frequently, in our quest to embrace tolerance of all ideas, practices, and ways of being, we overcompensate for the oppressive intolerance we face every day. With all the best intentions in the world, we swing wildly over to the other extreme and begin accepting every quirk and behavior no matter how outrageous or illogical it may be.

This is seen nowhere more clearly than on the Internet. I have a good friend who runs a rather large Pagan-oriented elist. A wise and learned individual, he holds some very heady ideals. Because his own beliefs are little unusual, and have often been judged harshly by others, he upholds the right of each and every individual on his elist to make any kinds of claims about their spiritual experiences, their abilities with magick, and their relationship with spirits and divinities.

No matter how ludicrous these claims may sound, no matter how deluded a person clearly may be, my friend will argue at length against anyone daring to question these beliefs on the basis that neither he nor anyone else can truly get inside that person's head to see exactly what they see. Given this, he argues, there is no way for anyone to make a case that any belief or claim to an experience is invalid. Anything less than this all-embracing attitude of subjective truth is decried as intolerance masquerading in the guise of common sense, logic or rationality.

Staking Wild Claims

I'm not sure how many people have experienced the amazing variety of spiritual claims that one can encounter within the

Internet. For me, it gets a little mind-boggling. I have encountered people who in all seriousness have proclaimed that they can cast a spell to allow themselves actual, physical flight. I have had more people than I care to count assure me that they own a copy of the legendary *Necronomicon* and that it is, indeed, bound in human skin. And that's to say nothing of the folks who have told me of summoning demons in the flesh, drinking pints of human blood a week, and being the living incarnations of their deity of the week.

I'd love to say that this is a phenomenon produced by the medium of the Internet, given how easy it is to masquerade as somebody else from the other end of a screen. However, in the days before the Internet, I had encountered similar claims. As I was dealing with people one-on-one or through limited written correspondence, the wild boasters seemed farther and fewer between. But the blessing and the curse of the Internet is that it puts us in contact with vast numbers of people. In this case, I think the percentage of wild claimants is a constant, but the sheer numbers of the Internet allow them more clearly to be seen.

I will say that the Internet does seem to encourage attitudes of uber-tolerance like those of my friend. In the past, I had no trouble telling someone point-blank I thought they were trying to put one over on me. On far too many elists, when I voice such an opinion now, I'm suddenly attacked from five different directions as being judgmental and simply not understanding someone's "different" point of view. Somehow the voice of reason gets drowned in a morass of political correctness and a misguided crusade to take freedom of speech to the limits of total intellectual anarchy.

The Trap of Relativism

There is a point where tolerance, practiced at the opposite extreme from intolerance, becomes something known as relativism. In relativism, there are no absolutes. Everything is subjective and relative to the experience and choices of the individual. From a relativist standpoint, I cannot argue that red is red because there is no way for me to adequately prove that *my* version of red is the same "red" being perceived by someone who may in fact perceive that color as blue.

Relativism caters to minority thinking in the extreme, careening perilously close to societal fragmentation and the disintegration of the fundamentals of language and communication. According to relativism, the very fact that someone *might* have a different experience than me makes it impossible for me to assert *any* experience as valid and true.

And here is the trap of relativism. When definition is based upon subjective opinion, how do we determine what is real and what is not? Concepts like "truth" and "reality" lose all significance, because meaning can and does change from person to person, depending on their point of view.

Relativism and Religious Diversity

Superficially, relativism seems like a good idea, especially where spiritual and religious beliefs are concerned. Acknowledging that experiences are subjective and that each person's interpretations of reality are relative to those subjective experiences is a basic part of accepting a diversity of religious beliefs.

Religious experience is exceptionally subjective. My vision of "god" is not a Muslim's vision of God, and even within a single sect, each person will have their own unique take on the divinity promulgated by that sect. But relativism, taken to its logical extreme, eventually allows someone to declare that "god" is in fact a dog, and no one can argue this claim.

Now, before I proceed any further with this argument, let me clarify my own stance on religion and spirituality. I am what I have often described as a Universalist. I believe that there are as many names for Divinity as there are people to speak those names, and even more still. Further, there are as many paths to Divinity as there are people to walk them, and again, even more still. Our experience of "god" and the universe is ours and ours alone, and it cannot help but be subjective, unique, and intensely personal, spoken in our own soul-language.

But isn't this relativism? And with such a tolerant worldview, how can one discern legitimate beliefs from psychological delusions? To quote my good friend and fellow writer, Jason B. Crutchfield, that's a slippery slope.

Truth Versus Delusion

In an ideal world, tolerance should not be qualified. In such a perfect and ideal world, the acceptance of every person's different spiritual beliefs, experiences, and practices should be absolute. But we do not exist in an ideal world, and as too many experiences on the Internet have proven, some people are just lying or are deluded about their spiritual experiences.

Most of us who have any experience in these matters have the ability to adequately discern a legitimate claim from a delusion or an outright lie. In most cases I've encountered, making this distinction is a no-brainer; we usually know on an intuitive level when someone is speaking from the heart about spiritual matters versus when they are shoveling a load of bull. However, if we uphold tolerance of individual beliefs as an absolute, there is no way we can really call these people out on their erroneous claims. There will always be that relativistic out that says, "Your experiences are not my experiences, so how can you know what's right or wrong to me?"

Usually there's no need to wrestle with these sticky issues of right and wrong in regards to personal beliefs. However, especially on the Internet, I have seen erroneous claims do a lot of damage. When people use the widespread attitude of relativism to essentially claim that god is a dog, a lot of newcomers who have yet to develop adequate judgment get themselves really confused.

In some cases, this just sets them back in their studies for a little while, as they have to backtrack from the misinformation and relearn the basics of things. In other cases, it may shatter a person's faith in everything once they have accepted an erroneous belief and then learned that it was based upon lies or delusions. In the worst case scenario, people are misled into really dangerous territory, as in the Halle-Bopp Comet group who committed mass suicide to join alien saviors in outer space.

The Slippery Slope

I have been wrestling with these issues for many years now. Despite my efforts, I have yet to come up with any hard and fast rules for rating the validity of someone's claims about magick or spirituality. Common sense is usually helpful, but within the Pagan and magickal communities, we are almost always dealing with uncommon experiences. I myself hold some beliefs that many would perceive as being "out there", and from a rational-materialist perspective, anyone who believes in magick is "out there".

The best yardstick I have found is not a rigid one. It takes into account the fact that individuals do have radically different experiences and perspectives, and it further takes into account that my interpretation of reality may not be accurate or complete. Going from there, I usually judge a person's validity based less upon their actual claims and more upon how that person presents those claims over a period of time.

Credible people tend to present themselves rationally and consistently over the long run. They frequently lead up to the really wild claims, often qualifying them and acknowledging that you might not believe and *are under no obligation to do so*. I am far more inclined to believe the apparently delusional claims of someone who tells me, "This is what *I* believe," than even the sober and reasonable claims of someone who says, "This is what *you* should believe."

The Middle Path

The very nature of spiritual experience means that much must be taken on faith. Of course in matters of faith, there is rarely an opportunity to provide cold, hard proof. When I do storm magick to end a dry spell, I have no way of proving that I was directly responsible for the ensuing thunderstorm. I just *know* on a level that often cannot be expressed in words. For someone coming outside of that sense of gnosis, the choice to believe is ultimately up to them – but at no time should a person feel obligated to believe simply out of a misplaced desire to respect my own beliefs.

The extreme side of religious tolerance tells us that we cannot disbelieve in anyone's experiences. The reality is that we should choose what we believe just as we choose which gods and goddesses to follow, or whether we follow any at all. Tolerating other peoples' rights to their beliefs does not mean that we cannot make informed decisions regarding the validity of those beliefs. The Middle Path of tolerance is when we respect and encourage diversity but respect our own judgment as well.

Spirituality and Generation X

As a minister who caters to alternate belief systems, I have had more and more young people coming to me to discuss non-Christian and non-traditional religious creeds. Now, some people would look at these youngsters and automatically assume from the way they're dressed or the music that they listen to that they are not religious at all. But this is hardly the case. Instead of a growing sense of religious apathy in youngsters, I've found that young people who belong to what pop culture has labeled "Generation X" have a very strong drive toward spirituality, and in many ways they are even more spiritual than their parents or their parents' parents. The only difference is that these youngsters lean toward spiritual paths that are much more open and multicultural than those of traditional Christian America.

Generation X is developing special spiritual needs to adapt to an expanding spiritual society. In a world made small by television and the Internet, Gen Xers are exposed to a myriad of different beliefs. It is not uncommon for these young people to go to school with Muslims, Jews, Hindus and people of other varied faiths. If they are raised in a strict faith which denies the validity of any other belief system, these young people are put in a difficult position. They can accept the strict interpretation their parents and pastors offer to them about the their "one true religion" but that means also accepting the fact that many of their friends follow a religion that is "wrong" and that these friends, through no fault of their own, will be punished by God for believing differently. The other option is to accept that there is truth and validity in all the varied approaches to God despite what they have been taught by their parents or priests. Either choice is a difficult one, but many Gen Xers are increasingly choosing to reject the strict interpretation that only one faith is correct and instead are exploring the diversity of many world spiritual traditions.

However, this more open-minded approach often creates a conflict between the children and their parents. Parents in strict religions who cannot accept the validity of other systems are often horrified that their children are considering other ways to believe. Parents and pastors alike experience a sense of betrayal because these young people somehow feel the religion they were raised in is lacking. While many religious leaders will insist that they are open to the possible validity of other religions, this stance is often not clearly communicated to the lay people of their faith. Just the other day I had a young lady come to me in great distress because when her mother found her reading a Buddhist text, the woman began crying, telling her daughter that if she did not believe in Jesus, she was going to Hell. It is a sad fact that many of the more open-minded youngsters, once they start experimenting with different belief systems, are persecuted by family and religious leaders alike. Their honest curiosity and innocent acceptance of other systems is condemned, and they are treated as pariahs in their families and towns.

Nothing could be more harmful to a child's blossoming spirituality than treatment of this sort. We are entering an era of unprecedented diversity and multiculturalism. The walls that had previously been built up between cultures of different traditions and beliefs are finally being taken down, brick by brick, and a dialogue has begun between people who, although they have radically different customs and ideals, are nevertheless unified by their common humanity. Certainly in our Christian culture, most of us were raised to believe that the Bible is the word of God. But in other cultures, there are many religious texts believed to be divinely inspired: the Vedas, the Upanishads, the Sutras, the Koran.

Our young people these days have an unprecedented opportunity to study all the varied world religions so that they can compare these beliefs and decide for themselves what they feel is most appropriate for their own lives. I think this religious multiculturalism should be encouraged, not quelled. If parents are really concerned about what their children may be exposed to, I strongly suggest that they read the texts along with their kids. If the whole family educates themselves about a different belief system, they are in a much better position to make judgments about it. Learning about other cultures and beliefs not only enriches everyone intellectually, it is also one of the best ways for us to break down the barriers that have kept our world fragmented and warring upon itself for so many thousands of years.

We have in this world many different languages, and as easily as many different names for God. At heart they're all the same thing, but it's a matter of learning to understand. I think it's a very good sign that Generation X is seeking to become spiritually multi-lingual. Through them, the world will not only be getting smaller. We will begin to understand one another better as well.

Revelation and Redemption: the Many-Faceted Jewel

I officially began my quest toward understanding in January of 1991. Prior to this date, I had often questioned the things I had been taught about my Self, my life, and the world around me. But up until that time, I had never had the courage to listen to the answers that I heard. As a result, I was miserable and confused most of my young life, caught in an inner maelstrom of conflicting emotions and beliefs.

Raised Catholic and reared in a very strict family, there were things which I suspected about my Self and about the very nature of reality. Yet these were forbidden things – ideas and beliefs that went against the grain of all that I'd been taught and expected to embody. I had fallen into a habit of intellectual fence-sitting: inwardly I explored my own spiritual possibilities while outwardly I embodied the religious conservatism which was demanded by my family.

Eventually, the cognitive dissonance became too much. I could not stand the kind of shackled, blinded life my situation was putting me in, and I wanted an easy out. I drove down to Whipp's Ledges near my home. This, I later found, was a spiritual hot-spot that practically every Awakened and nearly Awakened young person for miles around was drawn toward.

It was a place that figured strongly in their acceptance of their unique beliefs and experiences. And it was the place where I achieved my own epiphany on that grey January day.

The ledges are comprised of huge tumble-down pieces of local bedrock that were heaved up in a tremendous earthquake which rocked Ohio long before White settlers had even heard of the territory. The ledges were old when the Native Americans lived in the area, and if you explore the stones a little, you can see names and dates stretching over the better part of two centuries etched into their smooth, grey faces. There are enough signs of water erosion on many of the rocks to indicate that a lake once stretched out from the lip of the ledges, and other rocks have pebbles and sand imbedded in them, indicating that once they lay at the bottom of a lake themselves. Now, all that remains are the jutting formations of stone, startling to come upon within an otherwise normal-looking stretch of Ohio forest.

Even on an ordinary day, the sight of the ledges fills one with a sense of wonder. There is no denying that they are old. Age simply breathes off of them. And they seem to whisper of secrets, secrets that were dredged up with them in one monumental jolt of force that exposed a hidden part of the earth to the air and the light.

I walked toward this local wonder, meditating on the decision I was about to make. I looked back upon my life, my experiences, the things I believed. There was so much that seemed *almost* possible in my life, and yet outside forces always conspired to crush it down. I was tired of being crushed. As I walked along the forest path, working my way over the gnarled roots and intermittent stones, I prayed. I prayed to anyone or anything that was listening for a sign that there was hope and a reason to continue on.

The forest around me was utterly hushed. It was the dead of winter, and all the trees looked like blackened sticks protruding from the forest floor. The sky was leadenly overcast, and the forest around the ledges was heavy with mist. Everything was grey, colorless and grey and utterly dead. In my mind, the forest seemed a perfect reflection of the world I wanted to escape from: no variation, no possibilities, no sign of growth.

And then I came to the clearing where the ledges lay thrown out of the earth before me. And in the middle of all this oppressive grey death, all the rocks were alive and green. Moss and lichen stood out in vibrant colors against the grey mist of the forest, and a cardinal, almost on cue, fluttered down not ten feet away from me, his crimson plumes a startling contrast to the green-covered stones.

And it seemed that something spoke to me in that moment – the forest, the rocks, perhaps only the wind. It was a deep, non-verbal sort of communication, the kind of revelatory impression that just fills you up entirely. It spoke of freedom and of self-acceptance, and release from fear. I felt it wash over me, and suddenly every cell of my body seemed to thrum with that self-same vibrancy I saw on the ledges before me. In my excitement, I climbed up onto a large tree stump, threw my arms wide, and loosed a primal-sounding yell. It reverberated throughout the forest, sending birds in every direction.

I had come to the ledges to jump, but there upon the lichened stump, I flew.

My experience at the ledges freed me from the fear that had hindered me most of my life. I had been brought up to always worry about what others thought of me, but in that moment of primal ecstasy, I realized I didn't care. My life was for me. The secrets I felt burgeoning within my soul were mine, and I would do myself a great disservice if I did not accept them, explore them, and share them with the world.

In the years that followed, I studied a vast amount of material. I read the scriptures of every major religion. I familiarized myself with every myth, every belief system that I could gain access to. I studied various systems of magick and mysticism: alchemy, hermetics, shamanism, the Qabbalah,

Sufism – everything that was available to me here in the West. And in the end, I discovered that all sought the same answers at the core.

In the midst of all the gods and goddesses, all the dogma, doctrine, and ritual, there truly was a universal spirituality everyone seemed to be striving toward. It was the light and shadow of the universe, refracted to us through a million-faceted jewel. Some systems looked at only a few facets of this wondrous gem, some tried to encompass the entire thing. Some tried limiting the facets their adherents could see to suit some personal agenda, but even these systems were looking at the self-same gem. All systems strove toward it, none fully encompassed it, and the beauty of the jewel itself could only be appreciated by looking at it from every angle, every direction we humans could imagine – and even still, the jewel was *not* the shadow and light which illumined it. That was unquantifiable. That could never be touched.

But this jewel, it was the mediator between the unknowable and the known. Everyone could touch it. The major difference that separated the mystery religions of ancient Greece and Rome, early Christianity, Hinduism, and all the rest was the symbol system through which they filtered their beliefs – essentially, the particular facets each system chose to focus upon. Beyond the various names and stories, the details influenced by time and geography, the core of things was the same. All shared a concept of divinity which was humanity's attempt at naming the light and shadow they saw playing through the gem. All believed in the immortality of the soul. And all believed that this spiritual immortality was somehow a connection between man and the divine – that, when it came down to it, each of us was a facet our Self through which the divine light and shadow played.

Through this, I learned that the key to touching the divine force and allowing it to flow through your words, thoughts, and deeds, was simply a matter of realizing that it had been there all along. We are all gods, and God is all of us, plus the universe, plus all those invisible things we can neither see nor touch, plus something vast, something more. And my studies further taught me that the main thing keeping us, any of us, from accepting this fundamental truth is assumption. We assume that what we are taught in this world is infallible. We assume that we cannot find the proper answers for our selves. We assume that the world is limited to those things we can experience only with our five senses. We assume that divinity, by its very nature, is beyond our reach, and so we don't even try to touch it. We assume that we are powerless to change our world and our lives, and so we never make the attempt. Nothing limits us more than our assumptions.

That fateful morning on a grey January day, I abandoned all my assumptions. I died to my old way of living and thinking, and returned, reborn, to the world. And I came away with the belief that I *can* change my life, I *can* change the world, simply because I refuse to accept that I *can't*. There is much more to my Self and to my particular journey than that simple realization, but it is the first key lesson that everyone must learn. If we perceive that we have limitations, they are merely the limitations that we have set for ourselves. Once we realize that we can change those limitations, the very parameters of our reality can be transformed.

The Spiritual Evolution of Modern America Or, From June Cleaver to Generation X

What people believe, what limits they accept for themselves, and their attitudes toward authority and tradition have altered greatly in the past 50 years. The following is a very generalized look at three generations worth of belief which attempts to track the evolution of American spirituality from the simple acceptance of established dogma that I feel typifies the mainstream culture of the 40s and 50s to the open and sometimes bitter rebellion so visible by the end of the millennium.

My intent with this 50 year timeline is to demonstrate how we are all a product of our time, but as that time affects us, we in turn affect the future. Each generation learns from the mistakes of the previous one, and the second half of the twentieth century saw increasingly radical departures from accepted tradition with each successive generation.

There is a dynamic interaction here, and the current generation would not be where it is in terms of beliefs and attitudes without the effect of the generations that have come before it. I acknowledge that not everyone in Generation X has taken things to the extreme of the Gothic, Vampire, and Modern Primitive cultures, but the dynamics of belief and a need for a personal spiritual experience are evidenced even in the most conservative Gen Xers. The fact that they are seeking their individual truths in the religions of their grandparents does not, in my opinion, invalidate the fact that they are still driven to seek out something unique and personal that has been lacking in past generations' experiences of those religions. The expansion of acceptance and beliefs also still holds true for these individuals as Ecumenical movements continue to grow, and multiculturalism becomes a way of life in the 21st century.

Generation 11: Coming of Age in the 40s and 50s.
Significant events: Post-War Prosperity; The American Dream; McCarthyism
Ideological Reactions: the Rebel without a Cause; the birth of Rock and Roll; Invasion Paranoia
Spiritual Fear: Frightened by the possibility that there *might* be a deeper reality they can somehow affect and be affected by.

This is the era of our grandparents. It's a post-war culture with a booming economy following fast on the heels of a devastating Depression still alive in many peoples' minds. The National attitude is one of Idealism. Everything is A-OK in the US of A. No one has yet seen the dirt behind the façade, and those that do strenuously deny its existence – or are silenced. The religion of the State is Christianity, and attending Church is a function of family. To be a God-fearing citizen is the American Way.

People have been socialized to be acutely aware of their image, particularly as their neighbors perceive it. This paralyzes the dissenters and innovative thinkers into almost complete inaction. No one wants to risk the disapproval of the Joneses. Women, despite the hard-won right to vote years before, are content being stereotypes of themselves: June Cleaver wives and mothers, picture-perfect home-makers – and if they have trouble maintaining this façade, they drown the pain of their real faces secretly in alcohol, tranquilizers, and other pills.

To have a child out of wedlock is much more than a religious faux pas – it's a societal sin that earns both mother and child instant ostracism. Homosexuality is an abomination and a scourge, treatable by electro-shock therapy in mental institutions. Blacks go to the back of the bus. To be a good citizen, you must be happy, productive, Christian, heterosexual, and white. People who have different belief systems and innovative lifestyles keep these carefully to themselves. Some artists, musicians, and actors are allowed a little quirkiness, but even they might fall prey to the McCarthyism of the era, and have their individuality declared Un-American and dangerous.

Don't think that the need for individuality and change is not present in this era, however. The bright and cheery exterior worn by these decades masks some very significant problems. Looking back through the intervening years, we can't help but see that the smile on that blissful 50s housewife is forced and her obsession for a clean and presentable house is a sublimated need to achieve some amount of control over her life. There is a reason the UFO scare began and started to peak in this era. It's not because little green men from other planets were joy-riding over farmers' fields.

The invasion paranoia of this age is symptomatic of severe cognitive dissonance. Body-snatchers, Men from Mars, even the Communist scare all arise from the same fear of the Other. When you know that the face that you're wearing is a mask, and you know that everyone else's faces must be masks as well, how do you know what is really underneath? Eventually the façade had to crumble, and with it went a lot of our culture's ideological chains.

Generation 12: Coming of Age in the 60s and 70s

Significant Events: Assassination of JFK, Watergate, the Viet Nam War

Ideological Reactions: the Hippie Movement; Ecosophism; Pagan and New Age religions

Spiritual Fear: Frightened by the possibility that there might *not* be a deeper reality that they can affect or be affected by.

Americans pick apart the façade, and what they see scares them. We are not the all-good, all-powerful Empire of the West bringing civilization to other disadvantaged cultures. Our glad-handing leaders do not have our best interests in mind; the American Dream is revealed as a bitter lie. Our beliefs and practices are not the only ones in the world – we just seem to think they are.

Universities, those institutions of higher learning that the 50s era parents strove to send their children to because it was the Right Thing to Do, expose those same young people to many different ideas and points of view, effectively and irrevocably altering their perception of the world from that of their parents. And suddenly everything that was simply accepted as sacrosanct, from the One Truth of Christianity to the natural superiority of white males to the importance of a picture perfect All-American family, is called into question. This is the era where an education sets you free. And the young people of this time are ripe for it. Freedom of expression. Freedom from the bra. Freedom from stereotypes. Free Love.

Everything in this era is reactionary. It is the pendulum swing which must come in an equal and opposite direction from the 40s and 50s conservatism. Individual expression and creative thought have been so long suppressed, that when they finally erupt, it is in an uncontrolled and uncontrollable tidal wave of change.

Not content simply to explode the expectations of behavior their parents and society tried to ingrain in them, the young people of the 60s and 70s explode their own minds with LSD and other hallucinogens, striving to see the world from the most radical perspective possible. Radicalism is the word of the day. In reaction to their parents' unquestioned Christianity, the 60s and 70s people develop Witchcraft, Satanism and New Age religions. In reaction to American supremacism, multiculturalism is embraced and white youngsters try desperately to go native, seeking solace in any culture that is not that of their parents. In reaction to the patriarchal system epitomized by the wise and always-right 50s Dad, feminism springs to militant life. Homosexuals, bisexuals, try-anything-sexuals come teeming out of the woodwork in response to the sexual revolution, tending toward promiscuity in reaction to all those years spent in the closet or not even coming out to themselves.

Unfortunately, because so much of the change and experimentation of this era was reactionary, it was not carried out with sufficient forethought. Once the 60s and 70s young people got the pent-up rebellion out of their systems, the rubber band snapped. Uncertainty set in. Getting back to nature meant living a transient life of poverty, and too many baby boomers liked the creature comforts that their parents had nurtured them with entirely too much. Mind-altering drugs were all fun and games right up until the baby boomers had to deal with the possibility of their own children doing them. Radical feminism couldn't be maintained too strenuously if anyone wanted to settle down and have a family, so that got softened and evolved into the Working Mom. The promiscuity of the sexual revolution was severely dampened by the onset of AIDS and our culture is still reeling with the reality of that. And although many baby boomers still can't quite bring themselves to agree with every aspect of traditional religion, they still harbor a nagging fear that the Good Book may be the only truth after all, and none of them want to risk the threat of hell as they enter their waning years.

However, the Hippie era knocked over the pedestal, and everything that our culture had held in such high regard in the 40s and 50s would never be the same. Although a lot of baby boomers have inadvertently become their parents, their new-found conservatism has a hypocritical ring to it. This is a note that comes across loud and clear to their children. Their actions set a precedent for all future generations. While their parents were content to sit and sing in their golden cage, the baby boomers took a good look around and pointed out the bars. What Generation X must do is to escape the cage entirely and prepare our culture to get by on its own.

Generation 13: Coming of Age in the 80s and 90s
Significant Events: Corporate America; Reaganomics; the Internet
Ideological Reactions: the Gothic subculture; Body Modification; Extreme everything
Spiritual Fear: Losing the struggle to accept their awareness of a deeper reality within a culture that denies its existence.

The rise of the corporation has inspired the death of the individual. A person's worth is equated with his ability to be a productive member of society and fit within certain narrow parameters of behavior, attitude, and belief. Creative and innovative thinkers are actively discouraged, starting as early as in our schools. These become the problem children, the ones who, too intelligent for the system, get bored, slack off, and fall through the cracks. They are all given labels to explain why perfectly capable and talented young people do not perform up to par: Attention Deficit Disorder; Borderline Personality Disorder; Dyslexia; Bipolar Disorder – all of which are convenient excuses designed to put the onus of their problems on them or a faulty nature, and not on the system that failed them.

Many of them wear black all the time or piercings or freaky-looking hair in an outward expression of their intellectual alienation. And no school psychologist seems to understand that you can't make these kids fit in, the problem is they do not fit in, and we have eradicated the places that they would ordinarily go and be happy. With the quirky and unruly geniuses out of the way, the children that excel are the competitors and the over-achievers who blindly memorize the educational doctrine and vomit it back at their teachers for a gold star and a pat on the head. They will be good workers when their time comes. They don't know enough to question the role given them, and secretly the outcasts hate them for their easy ignorance.

Meanwhile, everything in America has become a corporation and a money-making business. Schools sweep the dissenting students, no matter how brilliant, under the rug so that the tax-paying parents and officials of the state can see a picture-perfect, well-adjusted and productive school deserving of more levies and grants. Hospitals are not interested in peoples' well-being. Treatment is based on level of insurance and the profit of the procedure. If you have no insurance, you are not worthy enough to buy your health.

Universities, once the Ivory Tower we all strove for, have become big businesses, too. Scholarships are given out not to the neediest or most deserving students, but to those whose statistics and scores will up the university's own statistics, so they can get a greater endowment of money the next year – they must prove their dedication to diversity, after all, and one or two National Merit Scholars balance out the dim-witted alumni children admitted to keep the donations rolling in.

It has become a regular practice of universities to alter the requirements in a student's senior year, changing and rearranging schedules so necessary classes are unavailable just prior to graduation and the student must return for a costly fifth year which is never covered by a scholarship of any kind. And the system learned its lesson well from the Hippie era; colleges are not places for free-thinking radicals anymore. They are places where future adults are indoctrinated in the beliefs and values of a materialist culture. And hot on the heels of all the angst and frustration that these other institutions inspire, the mental health industry comes to the rescue, marketing stability and happiness in the form of pricey little pills.

Anyone who has ever read Aldous Huxley's *Brave New World* should be terrified by this age.

We have become a culture of corporate clones, and we have been socialized to consume. If we don't have the money to afford all the expensive habits we're expected to keep, then the credit card companies will gladly help us out with a couple thousand here and there, regardless of our ability to pay. And then, over the next ten years or so, they'll squeeze tens of thousands of dollars back out of us, keeping us living from paycheck to paycheck just to cover the interest. And we cannot argue that the system was preying upon us when we were ignorant and weak. We cannot declare that it is unfair and wrong and in desperate need of change. There is no way to fight against the system and win – it is too firmly entrenched in the economy, in the popular imagination, in the very way America works in the 21st century.

In light of all this, Generation X cries out, "There must be something more!" But when no reply is forthcoming, we plunge ourselves into new extremes of behavior, struggling for any kind of sensation to affirm that we're alive, that we have an individual identity, that we have any kind of control. In our desperation, we assert ourselves upon one of the only things left to us: our own bodies, adding piercings, scarifications, implants, and tattoos. Yet none of it is enough to fulfill us. None of it grants us the uniqueness and meaning that we know must lie within our grasp.

We are clearly searching for something, but many of us just can't seem to figure out what it is. We want something radical and different, and the bottom line is we want change. Many of us have turned to magick and witchcraft to affect that change. Magick, whether it works or not, at least gives the illusion of control over our environment. In an earlier generation, perhaps we would have turned to prayer to accomplish this, but Generation X is far too individualistic and headstrong to rely upon prayer. Any changes prayer might enact would be made by a power that holds supreme control over our environment and our lives, therefore only serving to reinforce the feeling of our own helplessness. If we are going to achieve change, we want to have the satisfaction of doing it ourselves.

What it all means

If our parents chipped away at the pretty façade that obscured the harsh reality, our generation has not only looked upon but comprehended the bitter truth. There are some things in the world we have no control over. There are some things we cannot hope to overcome through direct struggle. This is not the famous apathy and fatalism commonly attributed the Generation X coming through; it is simply the pragmatic truth.

Our generation has no illusions of starting a revolution that will completely solve all societal ills. We already know there is no hidden button we can push that will suddenly make everything all better. Ideals are all well and fine, but the world is not an ideal place, and any attempt to make it ideal is doomed from the start. We could sit around in protest as our parents did and demand that someone change the system, but if this one is torn down, another will rise in its place, and eventually it will grow to be just as oppressive and stagnant. The very nature of a system, the structure and order it is built upon, means that it must stagnate in time.

We might not be able to change the system and save the world, but we can certainly change our selves. And it is through this direct and personal change that Generation X may find salvation.

By focusing on our own experience and finding a way to make every moment meaningful and sacred, we can rescue our identities from a faceless and uncaring world. By finding the path that awakens and enlivens us, we can fight through the despair that threatens to crush us. By celebrating our own individuality and creative expression, bravely and with passion, we free ourselves to realize the most treasured gifts of our soul.

We may be too suspicious and headstrong to seek solace in organized traditions, but that does not prevent us from seeking our own truth and applying it to our lives. The truth is everywhere. Sacredness infuses everything. We just have to look.

Once we have set an example with our personal strength and dignity, once we have made life choices that fulfill us and make us happy rather than grant us material wealth, when we have achieved balance between the sacred and the secular and re-instilled the wonder in our lives, we will create ripples that affect everyone we come into contact with. And in this way, and this way only, can we hope to alter the world and effect the change we know is so desperately needed: slowly, subtly, and one person at a time.

Pernicious Skeptics

Belief is woven into the very fabric of the human psyche. A religious sentiment – the need to not only understand the *how* of the Universe but to also ask *why?* – is not simply a quality inherent in humanity, I argue that it is a deep-seated human need. All one has to do to see this is to consider the implications of the archaeological discovery at Gobeckli Tepe. This religious site in Turkey is a human construction on par with Stonehenge – and it predates out very concept of human civilization. This is a mind-bogglingly significant find, because all of our previously accepted scripts for the development of civilization place the development of religion *after* the development of cities. And yet these amazing standing stones – many of which are inscribed with totem-like animals and symbols that could well be a precursor to a written language – these stones predate any known city. The monument at Gobeckli Tepe was built before any known cities and suggests, from its very existence, that cities grew out of religion. Long before our ancestors gathered together in permanent housing, they looked to the stars and wondered *why?* During a time when a massive effort must have been put forth each day simply to assure survival, a tremendous amount of time, energy, and resources were applied to a site that had no practical purpose but instead existed to quench the religious thirst that burns at the heart of humankind.

And yet, of all things, religion has historically divided us the most as a species. Cultivating religious tolerance is probably the only way to survive in a world that's turned so completely into a global village, and yet we still fight with one another, not only over religious differences, but even over the very fact of belief.

I respect peoples' beliefs, as long as they're willing to do the same. This means that I respect an atheist's right to believe in nothing. And I respect a true skeptic, who waits for proof before committing to belief. What I can't stand are pernicious skeptics -- those people who pride themselves on the equanimity of their disparagement of belief. They are always quick to attack the beliefs of others as foolish, naive, superstitious, or gullible. They climb up onto this high-horse of self-satisfied intellectualism, declaring that nothing is real save base materiality, and we should all be proud to inhabit a world divested of any possibilities. They would prefer such a sad, lonely, desolate world to anything that allows for mysticism, magic, or faith. Because, at least in their book, faith in the invisible (or even a simple curiosity!) is about the worst sin a person can commit -- especially if that person is smart enough to know better.

I call these people pernicious skeptics because they are *not* true skeptics. True skeptics simply wait for proof and, once they have proof of something, they are open to accepting that it is real. Pernicious skeptics rabidly seek to disprove everything, actually engaging in more mental gymnastics to affirm that the world lacks anything mystical than the believers engage in when accepting that it does. Further, pernicious skeptics are not content merely to disbelieve. They are driven to attack the beliefs of others out of some misdirected urge to save the believers from their foolish naïveté (or at least, that's what they tell themselves). They are the Jehovah's Witnesses of the faithless, Evangelically approaching any and every system of belief, from Christianity to Bigfoot, and seeking to prove the superiority of their disbelief. They treat belief as a fault, the ability to wonder at the vastness of the Universe as slack-jawed stupidity, and for those who entertain the notion that there is more to life than mere animal impulse, they reserve the greatest portion of disdain.

But pernicious skeptics are not trying to help guide believers out of the quagmire of their superstitions. No. Pernicious skeptics are not seeking to help anyone but themselves. They attack belief because they are offended that it can exist in another. They cannot sustain it in themselves, and thus, since their world lacks any sense of wonder, they must jealously seek to strip that wonder from the eyes of everyone else. At some point in their own lives, they were robbed of belief. This theft was perpetrated perhaps by an individual, perhaps by an institution, perhaps even by their own parents -- but whatever the case, the belief was, at the time, a significant portion of their foundation, the lynch-pin around which revolved their worldview. They desperately needed that faith, and to have it betrayed soured them on the very notion of faith. They are even now still hurting from that betrayal, painfully aware of the emptiness it has left within them, and their only recourse is to attempt to create the same emptiness in everyone else so that they do not have to consider the magnitude of their loss.

I see no functional dialogue that can be had with such pernicious skeptics. I am very sorry that their own faith betrayed them, but I think their attempts to strip the wonder away from everyone else are nothing but destructive. Believe what you want to believe, or don't, but do not attack, deride, or demean the beliefs of others under the guise of your own pseudo-intellectualism -- whether you are trying to convert us to a religion or to the utter lack of belief. It is fanaticism either way.

A Mirror Darkly:
Understanding the Modern Gothic Movement

Walking into the club is like walking onto the set of a horror film. Skulls and twisted metal candelabrums decorate the brick walls. Chainlink fencing defines the limits of the dance floor. Heavy chains hang here and there from the ceiling, calling to mind images of Clive Barker's *Hellraiser*. The lighting is dim. Everything is suffused with the otherworldly glow of black-lights. And wraith-like, pallid forms gather at tables and dark corners, their huge, haunted eyes thickly done up in shades of black, purple, and sometimes red.

They are a foreboding lot. Dressed almost exclusively in black, their patchwork fashions range in styles from the 1790s to the 1990s, covering virtually every era in between. Their dress can best be described as eclectic, with unlikely combinations of velvet and latex, leather and lace. Yet there is nevertheless a morbid kind of elegance to them. The waif-thin girls are pale as statues, their black-dyed hair teased into wearable works of art. The boys are easily as thin, with brittle, pretty looks that tempt one to describe them as effeminate. Everywhere, you can see jewelry and motifs more fitted to a funeral than a dance club. Girls and boys alike clutch velvet-embossed, coffin-shaped purses. Silver skulls glint from pallid ears. Necklaces with sculpted bats or elaborate crosses stand out upon thin throats. One can pick out spider-web motifs in the many bodysuits of sheer black lace.

But this is not a movie set or even a Halloween masked ball. This is a typical Friday night at The Chamber, a Gothic night club located in Lakewood on the West Side of Cleveland. Here, DJ Cable spins tunes by the Cure, Sisters of Mercy, David Bowie, Souixsie and the Banshees, and Switchblade Symphony. In softer moments, Dead Can Dance, Enigma, and Loreena McKennitt can be heard. To an outside ear, the music might sound strange, even unsettling. Minor chords prevail, and the lyrics overflow with sentiments of pain, desolation, and solitude. The club patrons, ranging from eighteen years of age to their mid-thirties, dance sinuously to their reflections in the mirrors that line the dance floor. Their movements are fluid, sometimes openly seductive, though rarely can two people be seen dancing together. Goths, inherently introverted individuals, almost exclusively dance alone.

I do not think I would be exaggerating if I said that no other modern movement has been as misunderstood or as misrepresented as the Gothic movement. The media has often portrayed Goths as Satanists. They have been portrayed as a cult. They have been scorned by righteous defenders of the

Christian faith as drug-addicts, sexual perverts, necrophiliacs, and blood fetishists. And most recently, they have been associated with the shock-rock star, Marilyn Manson, a comparison which makes most Goths bristle.

Moving around the club, one is struck at first by the outlandish costumes of the patrons. I can see where an ordinary passer-by would be frightened off by the funereal finery. It is tempting to judge on appearances only. But sitting down at one table, I quickly found myself surrounded by people who were friendly, articulate, and very much involved in the real world. Chris Robichaud, a graduate of John Carroll University, is working on a masters degree in philosophy. He is employed as a researcher at John Carroll this summer. When asked what attracts him to the Gothic movement, his immediate answer is "the darkness of it all ... the music, like the Misfits, that got me through my undergraduate years." Thinking things over he adds, "I think the Gothic movement is an inherently intellectual movement. Everyone makes the mistake of thinking it's just music ... It's so much more than just the music."

Asking around the table, it seems everyone agrees that most Goths were the brilliant misfits at their schools, those kids whose intelligence and vision alienated them from their peers but whose youth forbade them acceptance among their elders.

Forced to survive without a community, the Goths made their own, leading a solitary, introverted life rich in literature, creative writing, personal mysticism, art, and music. Most admired similarly solitary genius figures while growing up: Edgar Allen Poe, Lord Byron, Sylvia Plath. Separated from the main community of their schools, the Goths developed a value system independent from their peers, and ultimately their solitude led them to fall between the cracks of mainstream culture. Sports, television, and pop culture held little attraction for them, after all. They always sought something deeper, something which was both spiritually and intellectually fulfilling. Almost all the Goths were college-bound, and it was in that the larger, more cosmopolitan community of academia that they realized they were not truly alone. A large number of young people across the country and in fact world wide shared their likes, their dislikes, and their need for a deeper meaning to it all.

Next to Chris sits a young woman by the name of MJ. She teaches sixth grade at a Catholic school and has a degree in mathematics. Across from her is Jeff Gosnell, a waiter by day and a screenwriter by night. Shannon holds a job at an office downtown. I get the impression that she is a paralegal, though it's not entirely clear. Kevin is a social worker who has just been promoted to a supervisory position in the home where he works. Rich is an actor and musician who sometimes models to pick up some spare cash.

This small selection of people is representative of the club in general. Most of the patrons either have college degrees or are working toward them. Many hold perfectly ordinary jobs during the day. Almost all of them have some interest in the arts and have dabbled in acting, music, or writing. Interestingly, the professional Goths do not significantly alter their manner of dress for the work place. They admit that some of their fellow employees find them a bit eccentric, but on the whole, they are accepted.

Says Kevin of his position at the nursing home, "Sometimes I come to work and you can still see the eyeliner left from last night." He laughs, clutching his coffin-shaped hand bag with a demure gesture. "They don't mind the way I dress. I do my job well. That's the important thing."

In addition to creativity and intellectualism, Goths in general have a shared philosophy. It is hardly any kind of formalized doctrine. There is certainly no "Goth Bible" that everyone at the club has read and can quote chapter and verse. The Gothic movement is not a religion. It can most accurately be described as a lifestyle, and like most lifestyles, there is a wide variety of ways that it can be expressed. Some Goths do practice alternative religions, most notably Wicca and neo-

Paganism. Some Goths are also into sado-masochism. Some are gay. But these individual variations are not representative of Goths as a whole. The Gothic community is a very rich and complex social phenomenon which defies simple stereotyping. In general, their shared tastes in music, literature and art, has led the Goths to a similar world-view. To fully understand this world-view, it's helpful to take a look at what the Goth's major influences are.

Contrary to popular belief, Goths do not listen exclusively to so-called "Gothic" music. Although bands like Bauhaus, The Cure, The Sisters of Mercy, Lycia, and Dead Can Dance can be found in almost every Goth's musical collection, there are some surprises as well. Almost all Goths had an early interest in Classical music, and their current CD collections still reflect this cultured taste. Composers such as Carl Orff, famous for his "Carmina Burana," Mozart, in particular his Requiem, and Beethoven are often cited as favorites. Many of the Goths are also attracted to early polyphony and liturgical music, popularized by modern groups like Anonymous 4, The Hilliard Ensemble, and the monks of Santo Domingo. Music with a Celtic or Middle Eastern flavor also appeals to many Goths. Goths were listening to Loreena McKennitt long before everyone else learned of her through "The Mummer's Dance."

As far as literature is concerned, it is pretty much a guarantee that your typical Goth has read Bram Stoker's Dracula and Anne Rice's Vampire Chronicles. In the modern media, it is the Goth's romance of the figure of the vampire that has been most widely popularized and, at times, condemned. However, the Gothic taste in literature goes far beyond vampires. Goths seem primarily attracted to the poetry and literature of the 19th century. Poets like Byron, Keats, and Shelley, as well as Baudelaire, Wilde, and Yeats are often favored by the Goths. It is the Romantic character of these poets which attracts the Goths the most. Byron is favored for his melancholy, Shelley for his sublime imagery but also his anti-authoritarianism. The dark, often morbid tone of these and other poets, their fascination with the forbidden, and their mystical imagery also appeals to the Gothic sensibilities. Significantly, most Goths are also great fans of Pre-Raphaelite art, a movement which features sensual, idealized images, mythic and at times mystical themes, and a fascination for magic and the occult. Waterhouse's "The Lady of Shalott" is a typical Pre-Raphaelite favorite as are works by Dante Gabriel Rosetti.

Goths are certainly not Satanists, but the Romantic Luciferianism of the 19th century would have appealed to them, in as much as Lucifer is portrayed as the ultimate

Byronic hero. Milton's Lucifer, who was adopted by the Romantic poets as a kind of heroic symbol, was portrayed as an individual who dared to rebel against the established order and was cast out for his presumption. The Goths have stayed away from the controversial figure of Lucifer, but his identity as the Romantic outcast still appeals. This is where the figure of the vampire really comes in, for Lestat is clearly a modern counterpart of the Romantic Lucifer. Thus, for many Goths, the vampire has become their heroic symbol, a Byronic figure, whose fierce independence and individualism separate him from the ordinary society of mortals. Significantly, these same qualities also lock him on the outside of that society, forcing him into the role of the outcast, forever misunderstood and forever alone.

Most Goths acknowledge that they view themselves as outcasts from mainstream culture, but they admit that it is a role they have intentionally adopted.

"So many people stop and stare like there's something wrong with us," says nineteen year-old Stephanie, a Goth from the Ann Arbor area, "but we look weird because there's something wrong with them. We don't dress this way because we're freaks. We're trying to be a mirror, so everyone can see the darkness in the world that they always shut their eyes to."

This feeling of purpose is not uncommon among the Goths I've interviewed. Some Goths say they wear their black as a sign of mourning, like Barry Tessman, a graduate student in mathematics and sometime radio DJ. Barry feels a great sadness for the state of the world around him, and he has allowed that sadness to infuse his lifestyle. He is quick to point out that he is not depressed or suicidal, just aware. His is the sadness borne of wisdom. Goths like Barry are essentially in mourning for the world, and their attitude and dress is an expression of their inner feelings. If others notice this and realize what it really means, then so much the better.

Not all Goths feel their sadness is a bad thing. Some cherish it. What anyone else might consider depression, Goths perceive as inspiration.

"I hurt," says Joe, a sixteen-year-old Goth. "That's normal. Nobody can be happy all the time. But I write my best stuff when I'm sad."

According to the Goths, their more somber outlook also makes them more reflective. Introspection is a quality all Goths seem to share. They also enjoy their solitude. Goths are content sitting on the outside looking in. Outside observers often misinterpret their pensive moods.

"Everyone asks me, 'What's wrong, Dickens?'" observes Jason, a twenty-four-year old Goth also from the Ann Arbor area. "Nothing's wrong. Does there have to be something wrong just because I'm by myself, just because I'm not smiling?"

When you turn on the TV and see people having a good time, they are usually in a large group. There's conversation and laughter. Things are bright, cheerful, and loud. But this is the world of the extrovert. Our mainstream culture tends to overstress this "normal" party behavior. Healthy, normal people are people who happy. Most Goths aren't happy, but they are content the way they are. The individuals I've interviewed are all very aware that most modern psychologists would see their attitudes as dysfunctional and try putting them on Prozac. But they prefer themselves just the way they are. Once again, in keeping with their Romantic antecedents, the Goths feel there is a certain pleasure to be found in melancholy. It is bittersweet, but something to be savored nevertheless.

"Life isn't always good," says Stephanie. As a young person struggling to live on her own, she has experienced this first hand. "But the bad things have a purpose. We can learn from them. We survive. Darkness helps us appreciate the light more."

The more positive aspects of "dark" emotions is a point of much contention among Goths. They feel there is nothing wrong or unhealthy with feeling sad. It is natural and a necessary part of life. By pretending it's not, Goths feel that "normal" people cripple themselves. They don't know how to handle the darkness when it's forced on them in some life crisis. This attitude is also a fundamental part of the Gothic approach to death. Often accused of being morbid because of their fascination with death, most Goths defend their position as a more realistic one. Death is a taboo subject in our modern culture. It is something to be avoided at all costs, something no one feels comfortable talking or even thinking about. Goths have made death a part of their life. Symbols of death abound in their jewelry. They have a great love for cemeteries and cemetery art. Again, this is a conscious departure from mainstream culture.

Goths embrace death because mainstream culture shuns it. They feel that understanding death and one's attitude toward it is as necessary as understanding life. By turning a blind eye to death, "normal" people are once again crippling themselves in Goths' eyes. A whole person must be able to look at and accept the whole picture. That includes life as well as death, sadness as well as joy. This awareness of the whole is in effect the core of the Gothic movement.

"It is an issue of duality," says Lee Brown, a twenty-four-year old martial artist and a manager at a local office supply store. "People who are too hung up on the light fail to realize that darkness does not equal evil. Life is a balance of darkness and light."

Ceir, another patron of The Chamber, agrees with Lee.

"A need for balance exists. Just look at the world around you," he says sadly. "Goths have adopted the darkness as a balancing effort."

Again and again, I find that sentiment reiterated. Darkness is as much a part of life as light, and there is just as much beauty and inspiration to be found in the darkness as in the light. Perhaps more so, because in the twilight world of the Goths, beauty is a fragile and fleeting thing. It is therefore all the more precious when it is found.

"By dressing this way and being a Goth," explains Stephanie, "I'm telling everyone that the world's not just made up of shiny, happy people. And there's nothing wrong with that. Some of us like it that way."

The Goths are true children of the Millennium. In a sense, they are a symptom of *fin de siecle* decadence. Many of them have adopted their lifestyle in a conscious effort to make others aware of that decadence. Thus the movement can be seen as an intricate, symbolic, and largely passive outcry against the state of the world today. But there is more to the Goths than mere protest. They have a purpose and a vision.

They have sculpted themselves into living, breathing symbols of what they believe in. They dress and act the way they do not only in an effort to make people aware of the darkness, but also to make them realize that to a certain extent it is necessary.

These deathly-pale, black-clad children have a very positive message for us. Life is a balancing act between darkness and light. When we ignore the darkness in ourselves and in the world around us, that is when it becomes dangerous and gets out of control. But if we are not afraid to face it, there is much we can learn. Everything in life, good or bad, is what one makes of it. In this way, there is joy to be found in sorrow, contentment in solitude, and appreciation for life in the understanding of death. Despite their macabre appearance, the Goths are beautiful. It is a fragile, strange beauty, something we are not at all used to. Because it is alien, it seems threatening. But we cannot be afraid to look. The Goths are trying to teach us by example, but they are not going to spell things out for us. We have to look at them, as in a glass darkly, and understand for ourselves.

Balance in All Things

The universe is founded upon the principle of complimentarity. Everything is split into pairs of opposites, and it is through the dynamic interaction of these opposites that true creation begins.

The Western world has lost sight of this complimentarity. Our ratio-materialist culture is dreadfully one-sided. It's like a seesaw with all of the weight on one side: it's going nowhere.

The Pagan, Wiccan and New Age movements sensed this and tried to rectify it by rediscovering the divine feminine. But despite their best intentions, even these enlightened movements have fallen prey to one-sidedness. Most of the Pagan and Wiccan groups went too far in the opposite direction, favoring the feminine, intuitive side of things so much as to almost totally exclude the masculine, rational aspects. And even those that strove for more of a balance between feminine-intuitive and masculine-rational failed to extend that balance throughout all of their ideologies. All light and no darkness is just as imbalanced as all male with no female.

Mystical traditions the world over tell us that one of the greatest revelations lies in the union of opposites. The marriage of male and female, light and dark lay at the heart of the alchemical mysteries of the early Medieval Age. The visionary techniques of Tantric Buddhism hinge upon a similar mystical union. Rumi, the Islamic mystic and founder of the Dervishes, expressed it like this: "Nothing can be clear without a polar opposite. Two banners, one black, one white, and between them something is revealed."

Within the dynamic interplay of opposing forces, something that is greater than either of the two disparate poles emerges. In alchemy, it is the Philosopher's Stone, and this is a very apt symbol for it: it is that dynamic, subtle something that transforms everything it touches.

In my group House Kheperu, we seek this union of opposites as an internal state, working to achieve a dynamic inner balance between opposing forces in order to transcend and transform ourselves. In order to achieve this inner union, we understand that we must accept the existence of both aspects of the complimentary pair within our Selves. When most systems speak of self-knowledge, they are only speaking of the pretty and acceptable parts of our Selves. This denies and overlooks a whole half of our beings, and there is no way to achieve balance when in denial of this sort. Accordingly, we of the Kheprian Order come to terms with and celebrate our darkness as well as our light, our base desires as well as our noble ones, our irrational and emotive selves as well as our rational minds, and our existence as beings of the flesh as well as beings of spirit.

Even if we don't like what we see at first, we cannot shy away from the darker sides of our Selves, for without the darkness, we would not be complete. The balance that can be achieved by rectifying these various opposites is a dynamic and harmonious interaction, where we neither deny nor suppress any aspect of ourselves but harness it for a greater actualization of who we are.

Letting in the Dark: Gothic Paganism and Millennial Change

Wicca and Neo-Paganism are most commonly associated with the ecosophical movement which began in the 1960s. Although Neo-Paganism has much older roots than that, our most outspoken and activist-minded Witches tend to hail from this era. Unsurprisingly, this generation of Wiccans and Neo-Pagans share many of the same ideals associated with the hippie movement which they lived through. They are ecologically conscious, and their lifestyle is one that hearkens back to nature and the simpler ways associated with tribal times. They favor a matriarchal system and a social structure in which all participants share equally the burden of responsibility. And they are often polyamorous, or at the very least polysensual, rejecting the Puritanical morality of our culture and instead celebrating the body and its pleasures as something natural, beautiful, and sacred. In general, Wicca and Neo-Paganism can therefore be seen as religions of light, life, and love. That is, if you look only at the generation which arose from the 1960s and the direct inheritors of those Gaia-centered faiths.

Yet there is a new generation of Neo-Pagans. They are the children of the 1990s, the notorious Gothic movement of Generation X. Having attracted the attention of the press in recent years, the Gothic movement has been unfairly demonized by mainstream media. Talk show hosts and tabloid reporters have been drawn to the movement like the curious to a freakshow, and instead of depicting its diverse members in an objective and positive light, they have tended to blatantly sensationalize the Goths. In the hands of the media, Goths have become Satanists and necrophiliacs, delusional, self-proclaimed vampires and sexual deviants. While the negative image propagated by the press is largely unfair and untrue, the reticent, somewhat secretive nature of the Goths has not helped to alleviate the situation.

When it comes down to it, Goths are no better or worse than any other group of young people struggling to define themselves. In every social movement, there are a few attention-seekers and fanatics whose exploits tend to reflect badly upon everyone else. Ordinarily, the positive presentation of more rational members of the group serves as a counterpoint to the extremists. Yet, the Gothic movement is by nature something very dark, and this darkness inspires fear and misunderstanding even when presented by the most level-headed and respectable Goths.

The hippie movement chose to distinguish itself with extroverted revelry and bright, psychedelic colors. Although the appearance and dress of a typical hippie was a little wild and unusual, it did not possess the ominous look associated with the modern Goth. Goths favor introverted meditation and dark, somber clothes. They dress all in black, accenting their outfits with silver jewelry done in the motifs of bats, razors, and skulls. This image is admittedly intimidating, but part of the point is to intimidate. Goths not only embrace the darkness. They seek to embody it. They dress the way they do in a not-so subtle reminder that death and decay are everywhere. Many Goths consider themselves a wake-up call for all the shiny, happy people out there who think the world is all shopping malls and suburban kitsch. The Goth, with his painfully thin frame and his cadaverous make-up is screaming to everyone: suffering is real. Darkness is real.

The movement is not simply a rebellion against sterile, fake suburbia. Most Goths are also very spiritual individuals. Many started out in strict religions, typically Catholicism or Southern Baptism. Even in childhood they found they were in intellectual conflict with the teachings of these faiths, and they quickly drifted away, nevertheless seeking something to fulfill their need for meaning and spirituality. In adolescence, when they gained more control over what they could read and study, most of them found themselves drawn to Wicca and Neo-Paganism. These religions appealed to their need for an individualized spirituality, yet the Goddess and Earth religions still did not account for the darkness which the Goths saw reflected everywhere.

Deeply sensitive and introspective, the Pagans of Generation X are reacting to many of the same social issues that spawned the hippie movement in the sixties. They see a world torn by hatred and prejudice that is constantly, somewhere, at war. Impotent spectators of a tragedy they have inherited, they despair over the casual destruction of the environment and the equally casual destruction of the human spirit by corporations and big business. Yet, where the movement of the sixties was driven by an overwhelming optimism that there was still time to heal the damage and return to a healthier, more holistic way of life, the Gothic Pagans react most deeply to the sense that the final line has been crossed.

The Gothic movement is inextricably linked with millenarianism. While their mystical vision is not exactly apocalyptic, most Goths are reacting to the *fin de siecle* decadence and anxieties which have gripped our culture in the late 1990s. There is within the movement an acute awareness that times are changing, but in order for change to happen, old ways must decay and die. To such Gothic Pagans, this is very much the time when "things fall apart" and "the center cannot hold." Too independent to work together in groups, they nevertheless have achieved a unique sort of long-distance community dedicated to networking and disseminating knowledge and ideas. This is spread out across the country and much of the Western world, maintained through amateur publications and correspondence networks. By remaining as loosely and informally connected as possible, these new Pagans have created an extremely flexible structure of faith that will bend and not break in the face of a storm.

Immensely prolific, an entire underground of small publications has grown up in the past decade, each dedicated to the dark and somber style of art typical to the Gothic movement. Publications with titles like *Necropolis, Catacomb, Carpe Noctem, The Azrael Project Newsletter, Disenchanted*, and *Shadowdance* abound. Many of these do not overtly acknowledge the spiritual aspect of the movement, though the mystical content of the poetry and short fiction pieces is undeniable.

The *Azrael Project Newsletter* is one of the few publications to make the spiritual nature of the movement overt. Conceived by artist Leilah Wendall, this publication is faithfully dedicated to "a macroscopic understanding of the

Angel of Death" in all his myriad guises. The poetry and philosophic observations of the APN's readers are typical of the literature of the entire movement, overtly spiritual or not. In all cases, the primary image is that of death, a death which is not to be feared and reviled but to be embraced tenderly, unflinchingly. Death is often personified as a dark angel or even a vampire and through these anthropomorphic vehicles, it is depicted in romantic, sensual, and even sexual imagery. Through such metaphors, death becomes a mystical, transformative experience that should be embraced as a positive force of change and renewal.

Because this new generation of Neo-Pagans have chosen to embrace the darker aspect of life, they are often shunned by their older counterparts. Dedicated as they are to religious freedom and tolerance, most traditional Wiccans and Neo-Pagans cannot see beyond the black funerary trappings to the legitimate mystical practices beneath. But they are there and, informal as the movement is, solitary though each Gothic Pagan may be, there is an underlying unity to their mystical vision. At the core, Goths revere death – death as transformative change.

It is easy to look upon the sinister outer trappings of the movement and cast judgment. The Gothic Pagan does ruminate upon death and dying, possibly to a degree which may seem obsessive to the outside observer. His clothes, his music, and the character of his ritual are often somber, drear, or even macabre. This morbidity may inform his entire lifestyle, yet often its influence is subtle and manifests mostly as a serious mindset and a tendency toward introspection and solitude.

Yet, as observed earlier, these somber, reserved, and brooding individuals almost universally cultivate an intense creativity. The Gothic movement is not only a mystical movement. It is also a vitally artistic movement, yielding a wide range of poetry, artwork, fiction, film and music. This is the other side of death: its ability to clear the way for creation and regeneration. Is it any wonder that some of our most brilliant and prolific artists are the youthful ones who led brief and tragic lives? Death and darkness, rather than obscuring or eclipsing life, serve only to make it shine with a clearer light.

This is the truth that the Gothic Pagans are seeking to embody in their lives, their works, their very aesthetic: the darkness is necessary. Death is necessary, and we must look at these things unflinchingly if we are to understand them and control the roles they play in our lives. The Goth looks into his Shadow and embraces it. It is as much a part of him as is the light, and only as a whole and balanced being will he be able to survive the changing times ahead.

In all things there must be a balance, and in a dynamic system, the existence of two polar forces struggling against one another only increases the dynamism and staves off stagnation. Those who follow the path of the darker mysteries are the necessary and natural counterparts of those magickal workers dedicated to light and life. If the Goths seem extreme in their embodiment of these mysteries, it is only because the darkness is so suppressed within our culture right now. Even other Wiccans and Neo-Pagans tend to shut away the darkness, vilifying it and denying the crucial role it plays in their lives. Someone has to remind us that these forces exist and have a positive aspect, and as much as the Goths have chosen the darkness, I think the darkness has also chosen the Goths.

As a mystical system, Gothic Paganism is a very powerful tool to self-awareness and self-realization. There is no looking away from this dark mirror, even when all it reflects to you is your own face, decaying to a skull. The Goth, like the Tibetan Buddhist monk practicing the *Chod* ceremony, does not reject this image: he revels in the liberation it conveys. For the children of the 13th generation of America, standing as they are on the uncertain threshold of a new millennium, this understanding of death as a gateway to change and renewal is not just a choice of religion or lifestyle. It seems to be their birthright.

Brevity. Eternity. This Flesh.

Most people look upon death with horror because they fear that when the body ceases to function, that spark we conceive as "I" will wink out and burn no more. Recently, I saw a different horror reflected in another person's eyes: the realization that when the body dies, we do not cease, but endure forever.

Consider the source of this horror: After death, consciousness remains. Awareness remains. We perceive this world to a limited extent, and yet we can no longer participate in it. We cannot touch. We cannot taste. The essence of love remains, yet we can no longer embrace the beloved.

How many of us would consider that hell?

There are many systems in this world whose ultimate goal is the attainment of pure spirit. Such systems maintain that the soul becomes free from sorrow and pain once it is unburdened of the flesh; it achieves true immortality. And yet the pain of the body is a fleeting thing. The pain that truly lingers is our awareness of it - and that awareness is a function of "I" - that part of us that survives the body. We are immortal already, whether within or without a body.

Yet if we can carry the memory of pain along with us between our many lives, if the traumas we have endured in previous incarnations can manifest in phobias even now, doesn't this suggest that pain exists *in spite of* the flesh?

In spirit, our senses range far and wide. We are not limited by physical barriers or great distances. This may seem like liberation at first, and yet all the senses of pure spirit are ephemeral. It is too easy to lose context, then drift, directionless, in eternity.

Incarnation into flesh provides limits and boundaries. Limits lend focus and intensity to our experiences, and the necessary brevity of anything locked in time makes it that much more precious.

Is it any wonder that spirits who are otherwise timeless and immortal seek out incarnation into the flesh? We already know that on the deepest level, we are connected. What better way to affirm it than to touch cheek to cheek, lip to lip?

The Scripture of Chaos

Chaos is a word often toyed with yet rarely understood. Considered to be a force of destruction and disintegration, it was personified in myth as the demonic "Enemy" by most early cultures, an enemy which had to be subdued and conquered by the hero god, whether he be the Babylonian Marduk, the Hebrew YHWH, or the Egyptian Atum. In all these mythological cases, before civilization and even creation could properly occur, the chaos had to be brought under control. Yet even as the creator gods in these three pantheons had to overcome chaos in order to create, they also produced their first creations from the stuff of chaos. Chaos and order are thus inextricably linked, and the findings of polish-born mathematician Benoit Mandelbrot seem to strongly agree.

Mandelbrot is a rather unique figure in mathematics. The father of fractals, Mandelbrot's most significant contributions to the field of mathematics have been to our understanding of chaos. In his career, he has dabbled in everything from economics to seismology. Indeed, his apparently random bouncing from discipline to discipline may seem chaos-inspired -- but as with chaos itself, there is an underlying though not immediately discernible order which has dictated many of Mandelbrot's diverse studies: the pursuit of what we now know of as the Mandelbrot set.

The Mandelbrot set is essentially a map of an iterated function; it is a dynamical system, fractal in nature, which can be encoded within a very simple set of commands and yet contains infinite complexity and diversity. The equation whose solutions the set maps out is based upon a complex number. This is a number which contains both a real and an imaginary number in it, such as 4 + 3i. This number represents a specific point upon the complex plane where the real number 4 and the imaginary number 3i intersect. The loop of instructions which one feeds into a computer in order to allow it to map the Mandelbrot set takes the starting complex number and applies the arithmetic rule to it. As the computer iterates this function, working through the formula again and again, some solutions move toward zero and others move toward infinity. Those that reveal their attractor as infinity can be discarded, but determining which of the two attractors a given number may be moving toward is not always simple. In fact, it is at the boundary where "points are slowest to escape the pull of the set" (Gleick, p. 232) that the Mandelbrot set becomes most complex. At such boundaries, it is difficult to predict where and when a number will break away, and this unpredictability results in highly complex and intricate patterns which reflect the complex behavior of the numbers at the boundary.

These boundaries are what indicate the set's fractal nature; fragmented or fractured in appearance, they contain intricate patterns which twist and branch, radiate out from complex centers and curl into tight, sea-horse tail-like whorls. Even at high levels of magnification, the complexity continues. Indeed, increasingly higher levels of magnification at the boundaries only reveals an increasing intricacy in a pattern which contains constant echoes of itself and yet is infinitely diverse. The self-similarity of the Mandelbrot set further defines its fractal nature; within the set, there is universality. No matter how closely one inspects the set, it will constantly reveal new variations on its old form which, though unique in their own right, are unmistakably versions of the main set. In this way, the set suggests the microcosm theorized by medieval alchemists, a universe which contains infinitely smaller versions of itself repeated down to the tiniest imaginable particle and beyond.

Mapped out and glowing like a jewel with its many colors (arbitrarily selected to indicate boundaries -- black and white will do just as well, but simply does not create as visually stunning a representation of the set), the Mandelbrot set it fascinating to behold. Certainly, its intricate, diverse, and yet subtly resonating patterns suggest an order within chaos, yet it is really hard to appreciate the profound implications of the set simply by looking at its final form. To really understand all that the set and its attendant ideas about chaos and universal order imply, one must first follow the complex and meandering journey which led to the set's discovery.

Mandelbrot has written papers on a bafflingly diverse range of subjects. These subjects seem at first to have a little in common with mathematics and hardly anything in common with one another. They include an analysis of cotton prices over a 200 year period; the predictability of the annual flooding of the Nile; the frequency of earthquakes; the fluctuation of transmission noise in telephone lines; and even questions concerning the measurement of the coastline of Great Britain. Most of these have something to do with the gradual uncovering of the Mandelbrot set; all have something to do with fractals.

First let us begin with the fluctuation of noise in telephone lines. In his job at IBM, Mandelbrot was asked to work out a way to predict when bursts of noise would interrupt the transmission of data along telephone lines, thus causing errors in the transmissions. Such bursts had thus far baffled engineers, as they seemed to be governed by completely random laws. Only one thing seemed to hold true: the bursts of noise occurred in clusters, such that error-free periods of transmission would be followed by periods fraught with errors (Gleick, pp. 91 -- 92). Mandelbrot attacked the problem and soon discovered that it was nearly impossible to predict the average rate of errors; by dividing hours of transmission up into gradually smaller and smaller units, he found that the proportion of error-free periods to error-full periods was the same across the board. In other words, no matter how small the unit of transmission time measured, it contained the same rate of sparseness for the bursts of noise. The bursts of noise were infinitely sparse, separated from one another on smaller and smaller scales just as the lines in a Cantor Dust are separated. In a Cantor Dust, you begin with a line and then take out the middle third of the line. Then you take out the middle third of each of the two resulting lines, and so on, following the same rule ad infinitum. The result is a collection of points which are infinite in number and yet their total length is zero.

The Cantor Dust was something of an oddity in its day; the paradox inherent in its finite infinitude jarred noisily with the accepted concepts of Euclidean geometry. And yet here was the basic idea behind the Cantor Dust within the telephone line transmissions. For Mandelbrot, the appearance of something so clearly outside the realm of standard Euclidean geometry suggested that the vision of the realm and its concepts were limited. If Euclidean geometry dictated that a paradoxical thing like the Cantor Dust was merely a quaint oddity, then what was it doing at work in the real world?

A similar "real-world" paradox which seemed to go against the Euclidean standard was revealed when Mandelbrot turned his thoughts to coastlines. Delving into the research of Lewis F. Richardson, Mandelbrot discovered that the measurements of a fractal coastline like that of Great Britain varied a surprising degree. The reason for this, Mandelbrot asserts, is that such a fractal coastline is technically infinitely long. If one measures such a coastline with a yardstick, one measurement will be derived; but if one measures the coastline in inches or centimeters or millimeters, the answer will be increasingly large.

While one may be tempted to believe that eventually this number will increase until it has achieved the actual length of the coastline, Mandelbrot tells us that this is not so. Unsettling as it may seem in a Euclidean perception of the world, Great Britain, though it has finite area, is possessed of an infinite perimeter. In this, it is no different from the Koch curve or snowflake. This figure, another intriguing oddity along the lines to the Cantor Dust, begins as an equilateral triangle with sides of length 1. At the middle of each side, add another triangle one-third the size of the whole. The resulting figure resembles a Star of David. Continuing the process into infinity, one produces an object with an intricate perimeter whose length is infinite, yet the area of the entire figure remains no greater than the area of a circle drawn around the original triangle.

Such figures as the Koch curve and the Cantor dust are fractals; they are intricate and irregular and standard Euclidean measurements of length, depth, and so on cannot capture their essence. Yet as with the telephone line transmissions and the coast-line question, Mandelbrot began to see that such figures, although elusive to the Euclidean geometry that had been the rule for thousands of years, existed quite clearly in nature. Their existence caused Mandelbrot to question the essence of natural geometry. Clearly, mountains are not cones. Clouds are not spheres (Gleick, p. 94). Euclidean geometry is hardly natural, Mandelbrot concluded; irregular, fractal shapes are the rule, and within the rules which govern such shapes must lie the rules which govern nature and natural phenomenon.

The governing rule proved to be the Mandelbrot set and other sets like it; in his study of cotton prices, the data uncovered by Mandelbrot suggested the hazy outlines of the set. His study of the Nile's annual flooding, even of earthquake frequency, further suggested the dynamics at work within the

Mandelbrot set. In all of these cases, short-term fluctuations and long-term fluctuations had long been thought to be unrelated. In terms of cotton prices, economists tended to dismiss the fickle babble of short-term prices and isolate on the long-range changes which would hopefully indicate trends. Mandelbrot found that the trends were the same for both short-term and long-term periods. The smaller units were hardly freakish occurrences to be dismissed as irrelevant; they were intricately bound up in the same trends and processes as the longer units, just as in the Mandelbrot set, the whole of the set is echoed endlessly on smaller and smaller scales. The infinitely complex shapes of the Koch curve and the Cantor dust intersected with the irregular patterns in nature in their shared quality of self-similarity. At smaller and smaller scales, the figures remained the same (Gleick, p. 103). And it is through this self-similarity that the random processes gained predictability; long-term trends would resemble short-term trends, even when those trends were measured at increasingly smaller intervals.

In this way, chaos gives rise to an astonishing geometric regularity. Yet all the infinite complexity of the Mandelbrot set can be encoded in a few short lines of program. Highly complex structures and processes can be encoded in very simple commands, from the fractal geography of the human circulatory system to the equally fractal frond of a fern.

Mathematician and fern-enthusiast Michael Barnsley proves this with what he affectionately calls "the chaos game;" by taking a certain set of rules and then randomly placing dots on a piece of paper (or a computer screen) within these rules, complex figures can be drawn. Barnsley's example is a botanically perfect image of a black spleenwort fern (Gleick, p. 238). Chance plays its part in the placing of the dots; the process is random in that it is impossible to guess where the next point will appear. Yet there is order, too, in the fact that the parameters guarantee the same outcome every time. The implications for DNA are clear

This is the nature revealed by Mandelbrot: "simple systems give rise to complex behavior. Complex systems give rise to simple behavior" and the laws of complexity hold universally true (Gleick, p. 304). The scientific and mathematical worlds are still reeling with the repercussions of such a profound fact. To mathematician John Hubbard, "the overriding message was that simple processes in nature could produce magnificent edifices of complexity without randomness" (Gleick, p. 306). In Mandelbrot's vision of reality, chance is a tool; chaos is deceptive. There are always strange attractors at work, hidden rules which define the parameters for the world around us. Universality and self-similarity, long discarded as viable concepts for a perception of reality, are once more strongly asserted to be the rules which govern our universe. Yet it is the infinitely varied self-similarity of the Mandelbrot set at work, not the simple self-similarity which led Medieval thinkers to imagine human sperm as a fully formed homunculus, extremely tiny yet a perfect replica of a man. Mandelbrot, throughout his career, has written of chaos rather like an evangelist. His comprehensive work in the subject he describes as a "manifesto and a casebook" (Gleick, p. 104).

Despite many critics and persistent resistance to the ideas suggested by his work in chaos, Mandelbrot remains the final word in the area. He was the first to intuit its implications, and continues to be its strongest proponent, finding more and more diverse applications in fields from metallurgy to biology.

With its assertion of a universal order, of universality and infinite variation, it is surprising that Mandelbrot's work has not yet found strong adherents in the realm of religion. Ultimately, if what Mandelbrot's geometrical intuition has led him to turns out to hold true, much more than the secrets of DNA may be implied. If chance is indeed merely a tool of creation and chaos is indeed merely the guise of infinite geometric complexity, then we have come full circle and find ourselves back in mythology, where creator gods harness the primal force of chaos and order it into the created world.

What might be the ultimate nature of the strange attractor which dictates the behavior of the systems around us, within us? Could we rightly attribute to it a face, a name, a consciousness like ours yet existing upon an infinitely greater scale? For me as a Kheprian, Mandelbrot's work suggests the sort of panentheistic universe I prefer to envision. Some would even take the Mandelbrot set as proof of the existence of such a universe. While I hesitate to extend the analogy that far, I cannot help but wonder what new discoveries Mandelbrot and his understanding of chaos will lead us to.

Reality. Magick. The Nature of Will.

If you are going to use your Will to affect Reality, you must be willing to accept this fact: *As you create it, it creates you.*

To actively use Magick is to become a tool of the Magick -- but not actor *or* tool. You will become both at the same time, the tool itself and the active force that wields that tool.

This reflexive nature of reality is the one constant truth I have observed in all my workings. It can be stated in one simple word: Reciprocity. You have your ability to shape reality, because reality *wants* to be shaped. Your desire to change the world is merely a manifestation of the world's desire *to be changed.* One does not happen without the other. You are both the active principle, bringing about the change, and the passive tool that reality harnesses to change itself.

But do not mistake this for utter passivity -- your will is your own; your desire is your own. You will accomplish little if you are utterly passive, waiting for reality to work on you. Yet you will accomplish equally little if you attempt to be utterly active, trying to force yourself upon the universe around you. The state you should seek is neither active nor passive, but both at once.

It seems counter-intuitive but it is nevertheless true: surrender yourself to the Will of the Universe, and you gain the power to enact your Will upon that Universe. Active and passive. Both at once.

Duality is an illusion. The answer is always *all of the above, at once.*

Tolerance Versus Gullibility: the Politics of Belief

We all strive to be open-minded about one another's beliefs and experiences. This is essential to our community, because we have had to have an open-mind about our own beliefs and experiences in order to accept them as real and valid. Much of what we believe and what forms the foundation of our community's identity are claims of supernatural or psychic experiences that mainstream reality would seek to debunk. Our materialist, scientific culture has no room for a sixth sense, let alone a seventh or an eighth, and the empirical rule of science leads most materialists to assert that if you can't touch it, it isn't there.

So many of the perceptions and sensations that form a vital part of our experiences are subtle and numinous in nature. They cannot be proven in a laboratory. Often, it is very hard for us to "prove" them to ourselves. We simply have to accept that we are not crazy, that these impressions are valid, and that the materialist approach to reality somehow fails to account for a large portion of human experience.

Yet this creates a certain amount of credulousness within the community. Since we each have had experiences that the rest of the world would reject as lies or delusion, we are much more likely to listen with a sympathetic ear to someone else's experiences, no matter how strange they may sound. We are painfully aware of how hard to believe many of our own experiences and beliefs are, especially because we have had to struggle to believe them in the face of a culture that tells us these beliefs *must* be the product of a crazed mind.

Obviously, we don't want to disbelieve another's claims especially because we want to be believed ourselves. But this can lead us into a dangerous habit of accepting everything that is told to us by others without question, and the sad fact of reality is not everyone who makes an extraordinary claim is telling you the truth. There are quite a number of people who lie and make up tales about their beliefs and experiences. They do this as an attention-getting measure, to make themselves feel powerful and important, or to get you to follow them and accept further stories and orders without question. These are the poseurs and cult-daddies of the scene, and they hurt our community not only by preying upon the innocent and vulnerable, but also by giving the outside world a very negative impression of us.

So how do we know when our tolerance has crossed into the realm of gullibility? Whenever someone makes a claim to you of a supernatural belief or experience, listen carefully to what they have to say. See if what they say makes sense based on your own experiences. Even magick functions on universal laws, and although we may not understand all of these laws as of yet, they still seem to hold true in most cases. If what this person has to say is radically different from your own experiences and what you've learned of the magickal world, that should set off warning bells in your head. You should not discount their claims just yet -- it may simply be that your own experiences are limited and this person is discussing a principle that you have not encountered yet. It's also possible that some of the beliefs and conclusions you've drawn from your own experiences are either wholly or partially wrong. We make as a great a mistake assuming that everything we believe is 100% accurate as when we believe that everything other people tell us is 100% accurate.

After analysing what the person has to say, analyse the person himself. How does he act? How does he dress? Does he speak like someone who is reasonably intelligent and well-educated? These might sound like judgments based on superficial things, but the fact of the matter is that mentally unbalanced individuals often demonstrate their problems in their mannerisms, diction, and dress. Not everyone who has a nervous tic is insane, just as not everyone who refuses to look you in the eye is lying to you, but these are good cues to keep in mind when trying to judge someone's credibility. There are quite a lot of people who our mainstream culture would label depressed or bipolar or delusional who have had very legitimate experiences and who have a lot of insightful and worthwhile things to say. However, you must keep in mind that people with chemical imbalances and unstable personalities cannot always determine the line between reality and imagination, and any of their stories should be especially scrutinized for this reason.

After analyzing the person, analyze the situation in which you are receiving this information. What could the person's motivation for speaking with you be? What kind of level of trust has been built up between you? Chances are, the voodoo queen of Wheeling would not come right out and say who she is and what kind of army of zombies she commands to every Tom, Dick, and Harry on the street. Common sense dictates that she'd have to trust you quite a bit to reveal information as sensitive as that, and if you just met someone at a coffee house who makes similarly wild and powerful claims, chances are, they're telling you a tall tale.

If it's pretty clear that the person making the claim has something to gain from you be very leery of it. But also keep an open mind on what you consider "gain" to be. Not everyone who's trying to "sell" you something is out for your money. A lot of people are simply motivated by a need to be believed, or they want to get you on their "side" for some imagined conflict. If you thought you left the petty social politics and cliqueishness behind in high school, you're in for a surprise, because as far as I've noticed, those silly social games keep a lot of people occupied well into their 70s.

Sex is another basic motivator, and if you're a pretty young girl (or even a pretty young boy), really keep your eyes open when people start coming up to you and trying to tell you how the universe works. All too often, they'll wind up trying to teach you tantric sex magick or something similar -- the long and the short of it is they want you in their bed.

With all these things to watch out for, how can you ever find a teacher or mentor that you can trust? Well, the best approach is to educate yourself. There are a lot more books out there than used to be the case, and with the Internet, a great deal of material is at your very fingertips. Not everything in a book or on a web page is truthful or accurate -- just about everyone is trying to sell you something in this day and age. However, if you approach all information cautiously, analyse it carefully in respect to your own experiences, and try to judge the motivations of the writer, you'll find a lot to teach yourself.

Material that you read in a book or on a webpage is a little safer than having someone come up to you and spout off all their vast occult knowledge. For one thing, you can read at your leisure, and if there are claims or references in the work that set off alarm bells for you, you have the additional luxury of being able to research those claims and see what other authorities have to say about them. Also, although part of a writer's job is to present a convincing argument so you agree with his points, still read material is not nearly as dynamic nor as potentially overwhelming as spoken conversation delivered by a real pro at the debating game. So when you're just starting out and you're not sure what to believe or who to believe it from, read, read, read! It will give you a great background for later when you are comfortable enough and self-assured enough to tackle face to face conversations with people who may be trying to take advantage of you.

For face to face conversations and study, always try to stick with informal study groups where everyone has an equal say. You'll find that some persons within the group can be considered authorities on certain topics, but as long as they're not always trying to dictate what others will accept and believe, then they're the kinds of authorities that will only help you expand your own knowledge. Steer clear of groups or individuals who are "gathering members for a light and darkness war" or who are engaged in "battles on the astral plane" or other such nonsense. These psychic war dialogues are just a very common and dramatic way to pull people into the group, incite them with a purpose, and let them run around as pawns for one or more cultish-type leaders.

Also, if someone comes up to you and claims to have information for you because they've known you in a past life, try to make certain that you get impressions that reinforce what this individual is saying. That's another dialogue that I've seen misused in groups in the past, and unfortunately many a poor innocent has had her head screwed on backwards with tall tales of a long ago life in a magickal time that's nothing more than a tale someone was spinning to gain her affection.

So, back to tolerance and gullibility. There is nothing wrong with listening to what people have to say. In fact, I encourage everyone to keep an open mind, because we can never be 100% certain that our own beliefs are entirely accurate or well-founded. Even if a person you talk with has beliefs you utterly disagree with, still you've learned something in the very act of ordering your thoughts for conversation and comparing your beliefs against their own.

Do not, however, believe everything that is told you. You should not go around being paranoid of everyone who comes up to you and wants to chat about spiritual things, but you should let wisdom and common sense guide you. Always analyse what the person is saying to you, analyse the person himself, and analyse the situation and what may be gained from getting you to believe the story. If any of these things set alarm bells off for you, then take what is said with a grain of salt. Feel free to challenge someone's beliefs that you disagree with -- sometimes there's nothing better than a heated debate on theology. And if they are unwilling to debate or defend their beliefs to you, or to back up their claims with real incidents or examples, you can probably spend your time better with someone else.

The Fractal Nature of Magick

I have a confession to make. I don't believe in magick.

That's not to say that I don't think certain people – and perhaps even *all* people – can shape reality with their Will, especially when they really work at it. But I don't believe that's magick. In fact, I think that's just the nature of reality. Calling it magick over-mystifies it, almost implying that we cannot ever know it and cannot really control it. In my mind, what we call magick is a natural part of the universe that functions on knowable, measurable rules.

I took a course in Chaos Theory when I was in college, and that made it all make sense to me. Everything is a fractal. Reality itself is a fractal. It all functions on the principles of chaos theory, which basically tells us that absolutely random events *do* have a pattern – we just can't see it because we're too close to the individual events.

How does this work and how does it relate to magick? By now I'm sure everyone is familiar with the example of the butterfly. A butterfly flaps its wings off the coast of the Philippines. A few days later, there is a hurricane off the coast of Florida. These two events are linked, but the link is present through such a non-linear chain of events that no one in his right mind would ever suspect that the cause of the hurricane was, in fact, the butterfly.

But by the principles of chaos theory, butterfly equals hurricane. Not every time. It might be mouse equals hurricane or speck of dust equals earthquake. The relation is non-linear. It is nearly impossible to discern. But the important part here, the real revelation, is who would think a butterfly could affect reality in such a profound way? Who would think that a person, just in *wanting* something to happen, could affect reality in such a profound way?

The chain of events is indeed non-linear, but I think in many cases the desire, the thought, the sympathetic action is all the butterfly we need. In that sense we are all butterflies, and reality is determined through such a complex interweaving of our thoughts and actions – even those tiny, insignificant actions that we cannot imagine will have any repercussion whatsoever – that it *looks* like magick. What else can you call it?

I do a lot of storm magick. I might as well call it magick, as that's the most convenient term for getting my meaning across. But to define briefly what I mean when I say magick, let's say x = magick where magick is the act of affecting reality through a non-linear chain of events whose first cause is a non-physical exercise of will.

But to return to storm magick. I think weather is the ultimate fractal that our tiny little random effects can influence. I don't believe that I and I alone determine the weather in my area. I think that absolutely every person alive influences the weather. Just about everybody *tries* to influence the weather. Some people want it to be sunny and clear, some people want rain, some people want it hot, some people want it hotter… Here are all these random little variables that get plugged into the fractal equation that gives us the weather. And after all of these little wishes, desires, and prayers have been factored in, you get the pattern that emerges – thunderstorms one day, clear skies the next, and Thursday a tornado.

Who made the weather? Just because I got my thunderstorms, I'll assume that I did, but I certainly didn't do it alone. Mine was one Will acting upon reality in the face of many, many Wills. Now, not all of those individual Wills came from people who really believed that they could affect the weather. Not all of those desires were completely focused and uttered with intent. So maybe those butterflies didn't flap their wings hard enough to stir up the right dust. Maybe a butterfly who *knows* he can flap his wings and change the world has a little more impact than the rest. Who knows? The end result is, I get the weather patterns I like nine times out of ten. I don't really care how it happens, just that it works.

Of course, this has always brought up the question of was I the sword, or the man wielding the sword? Plainly speaking, did the weather pattern happen because I wanted it to, or did I want it because that weather pattern needed to happen?

Here's where we get into the really mind-boggling complexity of the reflexive nature of reality. My answer is both. I wanted it to happen because it needed to happen *and* it happened because I wanted it to happen.

To make any sense of this, you have to have some familiarity with a fractal. I prefer the Mandelbrot set. It's a beautiful, beautiful thing. Fractals are the embodiment of the Hermetic doctrine, as above, so below. A fractal has an overall pattern that we can perceive, but what were are looking at, even in the Mandelbrot set, is just one tiny part of the set. The fractal itself is infinite. There is no end to the random series of numbers that you can plug into the function that makes it. The pattern gets bigger and bigger until it is so big you cannot conceive it, and the fractal gets smaller and smaller, until it is so small you cannot conceive it. And on every single one of those vast and infinite levels, the same pattern is repeated, over and over again. With one catch. The pattern, although similar, is never identical. Never. It repeats itself with infinite variations on infinitely smaller and larger scales. It's reality.

So within the scope of a pattern so complex, something which manifests out of apparent total chaos, it is entirely feasible that the person wielding the sword is at the same time that he is wielding it, the sword itself. He is actor *and* action *and* tool.

So as for magick – why wouldn't it work? Isn't it the nature of reality? Everything in the world functions on a fractal, from seismic activity to the way the branches of a tree grow, to the pattern of bronchioles in your lungs, to the pattern of nerves and of blood vessels in your body. Fern leaves – yep, the shape of those are determined by a fractal. There's even a neat little equation you can find that you can run through one of those new fangled calculators that will plot points out, and eventually, after many repetitions of the function, you will see the exact pattern of a fern. (see James Gleick's book on *Chaos* for that one)

So what this all boils down to is this: reality is a hell of a lot more complex than we give it credit for, and yet it is also a hell of a lot simpler to affect. There are rules, but you don't even need to understand those rules to use them. A baseball player uses calculus every time he throws the ball, but that doesn't mean he has to actually figure out all those equations in his head. A cat uses calculus to judge the distance of a jump and land with that astonishing feline grace, but you certainly won't see kitty in math class, writing out equations on the board.

You don't have to understand it to make it work for you. Do something, and the world will react. You can call it magick or prayer or miracles or anything you want to. What you call it doesn't matter. What matters is the pattern, and as we are all a part of that pattern, we cannot help but participate in giving that pattern shape in the world.

Imagination and Reality

Everything we imagine is real.

Thought creates energy, and energy shapes reality. One thought, unfocused, is but a tiny pebble cast into the universal sea. But what of those dreams and stories in which we long to believe?

In ages past, we had gods and goddesses. Whole cultures were told their stories, their life-histories, and rehearsing these, believing these, our ancestors added to their power.

In this materialist age, our myths are different. We encounter them in the pages of a novel, in a comic, on the screen. We may not revere them as sacred or god-like, but think how many more minds are brought in to focus upon them, all at once, through the media which connects most of the known world.

Think of how many minds yearn toward the reality of a Middle-Earth, an Arakis, a Neo when such archetypal images stir us to the depths of our souls, even for but a moment, when they captivates us on the screen.

How many minds, yearning, does it take to create a tidal wave? And will we be surprised when we come face to face with the new beings that we have made?

Works Cited

There are several works cited in my thesis on shamanism. Unfortunately, I originally saved the bibliography for this paper in a separate file. That separate file has been lost. While I have been able to identify the majority of works cited in that paper, as I still own the books, at least two are unaccounted for. I have not been able to identify the work by Schmidt. The work by Noll was a paper comparing shamanism and schizophrenia, but I no longer have the full citation for that paper. Nevertheless, I have left the parenthetical notations within the text and provide titles here as best I can:

Achterberg, Jeanne. *Imagery in Healing: Shamanism and Modern Medicine*

Eliade, Mircea. *Shamanism: Techniques of Ecstasy.*

Drury, Nevill. *The Shaman and the Magician.*

Gleick, James. *Chaos: Making a New Science.*

Harner, Michael. *Way of the Shaman.*

Hultkrantz, Ake. *The Religions of the American Indians.*

Kalweit, Holger. *Dreamtime and Inner Space.*

Noll, Richard.

86342959R00137

Made in the USA
Columbia, SC
12 January 2018